The Bridge Player's Alphabetical Handbook

by the same authors

―――

THE COMPLETE BOOK OF BRIDGE
(Faber and Faber)
THE ACOL SYSTEM OF BIDDING
(Robert Hale and Pan Books)
THE PLAY OF THE CARDS
(Robert Hale and Sphere Books)
BRIDGE FOR TOURNAMENT PLAYERS
(Robert Hale)
HOW TO PLAY A GOOD GAME OF BRIDGE
(Heinemann and Pan Books)

The Bridge Player's Alphabetical Handbook

TERENCE REESE
and
ALBERT DORMER

FABER AND FABER
London · Boston

First published in 1981
by Faber and Faber Limited
3 Queen Square London WC1N 3AU
Photoset by Western Printing Services Ltd, Bristol, England
Printed in the United States of America
by the Maple-Vail Book Mfg. Group, New York

British Library Cataloguing in Publication Data

Reese, Terence
The bridge player's alphabetical handbook.
1.Contract bridge – Dictionaries
I. Title II. Dormer, Albert
795.4′15′03   GV1282.22

ISBN 0–571–11599–3

Contents

Foreword

Our objective in this book has been to give a concise but comprehensive account of all aspects of the modern game, excluding only some of the specialized conventions employed by small groups of tournament players. In so far as the two can be separated, our principle has been to inform rather than to instruct. Our policy in respect of the main subjects has been as follows:

Bidding methods, systems and conventions. We have covered the general framework of bidding in terms of such headings as opening bids, responses, pre-emptive bids and the like. Where there is a notable difference between British and American style, we have described both. All the better known systems and conventions have been included. Obviously it would not have been practical to describe *all* the conventions used by tournament players. These come and go by the dozen every month. We have had to distinguish between established conventions and passing fashion.

Play. Here we explain the meaning of all the familiar terms and stratagems, such as ducking, squeeze, elimination and the rest. We describe all popular systems of leads, signals and conventions in play.

Laws. The account of the Laws is not exhaustive but is designed to cover all normal occurrences. Distinctions are noted between the 1963 code for rubber bridge and the 1975 code for duplicate.

Tournament procedure. We describe the terms that arise in tournament play and explain the commoner forms of duplicate movement; but we do not aim to provide a tournament director's handbook.

Definitions. We explain a number of terms that are part of the game but are not connected with technical accomplishment.

We want this Handbook to be as useful and complete as possible. With a view to future editions, we shall be pleased to hear from any reader who has a reasonable question, not concerned with some esoteric convention, to which he cannot find the answer.

Guide to Entries

The book is divided into three parts: Bidding; Play; Laws, Tournament Procedure and Definitions. The entries are in alphabetical order within each part, but to narrow the search for a reader who wishes to examine a particular branch of the game, this Guide is divided into smaller sections.

Bidding

1. Standard bidding
2. Valuation
3. Tactical manoeuvres
4. Systems
5. Conventions

Play

6. Leads
7. Signals and conventions
8. Tactical moves in the middle game
9. End game technique

Laws, Tournament Procedure and Definitions

10. Laws
11. Tournament procedure
12. Definitions

A few titles appear under more than one heading. For example, the Losing Trick Count is both a method of valuation and a system of bidding. Where there are alternative names for the same subject, both are listed.

BIDDING

1. Standard bidding

Biddable suits – Delayed game raise – Double raise of suit opening – Doubles – False preference – Forcing bid – Fourth suit forcing –

Free bid, raise and rebid – Free double – Informatory double – Jump overcall – Jump preference – Jump raise – Jump rebid – Jump shift – Mathematics of rubber bridge – Moysian fit – Notrump overcall – Notrump response to suit opening – One-notrump opening – Opening suit bids of One – Overcall – Part-score bidding – Passed hand – Penalty double – Penalty pass – Positive response – Pre-emptive bid – Preference bid – Prepared bid – Psychic bid – Quantitative 4 NT – Rebids by opener – Redouble – Relay bid – Responses to opening bids of one – Reverse bid – Short club – Sign-off bid – SOS redouble – Take-out double – Third-hand opening – Three bid – Three-notrump opening – Three notrump take-out – Trap pass – Trial bid – Two-club opening – Two-diamond opening – Two-notrump opening – Weak jump overcall – Weak notrump – Weak two-bid.

2. Valuation

Distributional point count – Duplication of values – Honour tricks – Losing trick count – Milton Work count – Playing tricks – Point count – Rule of two and three.

3. Tactical manoeuvres

Advance cue bid – Advance sacrifice – Balancing – Competitive doubles – Controls – Co-operative double – Cue bid by opening side – Cue-bid overcall – Cue bid to show controls – Defence to 1 ♣ bids – Directional asking bid – Five-card majors – Forcing 1 NT response – Forcing pass – Fourth-hand opening – Fourth suit forcing – Game-forcing overcall – Lead-directing doubles – Lead-inhibiting bids – Negative double – Optional double – Phantom sacrifice – Principle of fast arrival – Protective bid – Responsive double – Short club – Short-suit game tries – SOS redouble – Sputnik – Trap pass – Trial bid – Unassuming cue bids – Unpenalty doubles.

4. Systems

Acol – Baron – Blue Club – CAB – Carrot Club – Culbertson – EFOS – Flint-Pender – Forcing two – Goren – Kaplan-Sheinwold – Little Major – Losing trick count – Neapolitan – Nottingham – One club – Precision – Roman – Romex – Roth-Stone – Vienna.

5. Conventions

Ace-showing responses to 2 ♣ – Asking bids – Astro – Astro cue bid

– Baron grand slam try – Baron 2 NT response – Benjamin – Blackwood – Brozel – Byzantine Blackwood – Canapé – Cansino defence – Conventions – Crowhurst – Culbertson 4–5 NT – Declarative-interrogative 4 NT – DEPO – DOPI – Drury – Exclusion bid – Fishbein – Five-ace Blackwood – Flannery 2 ◊ (or 2 ♡) – Flint – Forcing two-bids – Four-club Blackwood – Four notrump opening – Fragment bid – Gambling 3 NT – Gardener notrump overcall – Gerber – Gladiator – Grand slam force – Herbert – Inverted minor suit raises – Kock-Werner redouble – Landy – Lebensohl – Lightner double – Lower minor – Michaels cue bid – Mini-notrump – Multicoloured 2 ◊ – Negative double – Ogust rebids – PODI – Psychic controls – Relay bid – Ripstra – Roman Blackwood – Roman jump overcalls – Roman 2 ◊ – Sharples 4 ♣ – Short-suit game tries – SNAP – Splinter bid – Sputnik – Stayman – Texas – Three notrump take-out – Transfer bids – Trump asking bids – Two-club opening – Two-diamond opening – Unpenalty doubles – Unusual notrump – Weak two-bid.

PLAY

6. Leads

Ace from ace-king – Attacking lead – Attitude signals – Buso – Deceptive lead – Journalist leads – Leads against notrumps – Leads against trump contract – MUD leads – Opening lead – Roman leads – Rusinow leads – Top-of-nothing lead.

7. Signals and conventions

Attitude signals – Benjamin trump signal – Echo – Lavinthal discards – McKenney convention – Odd-even signals – Peter – Reverse signals – Roman (odd-even) signals – Signalling – Smith peters – Suit-preference signal – Trump echo – Vinje trump signal.

8. Tactical moves in the middle game

Anti-percentage play – Assumption – Avoidance play – Backward finesse – Bath coup – Blocking play – Combination finesse – Communication play – Counting the hand – Covering honours – Crashing honours – Crossruff play – Deschapelles coup – Discovery – Double finesse – Ducking – Dummy reversal – Echelon play – Entry-killing play – False-carding – Finesse – Finesse against dummy – Finesse against partner – Forcing tactics – Grosvenor

Coup – Hold-up play – Intra-finesse – Loser-on-loser play – Merrimac coup – Morton's Fork – Optimum strategy – Probabilities of distribution – Restricted choice – Reverse dummy play – Ruffing finesse – Rule of eleven – Safety play – Scissors coup – Symmetry of distribution – Tempo – Tenace – Trump control – Trump promotion – Two-way finesse – Unblocking play – Uppercut – Waiting move.

9. End game technique

Automatic squeeze – Coup – Coup de l'agonie – Coup-en-passant – Criss-cross squeeze – Crocodile Coup – Defending against squeezes – Devil's coup – Double squeeze – Elimination – End play – Grand coup – Guard squeeze – Menace – Overtaking squeeze – Progressive squeeze – Pseudo-squeeze – Rectifying the count – Ruff-and-discard – Smother play – Squeeze play – Squeeze without the count – Submarine squeeze – Suicide squeeze – Threat – Throw-in – Trump coup – Trump squeeze – Vienna coup.

LAWS, TOURNAMENT PROCEDURE AND DEFINITIONS

10. Laws

Bid – Bid out of turn – Call out of turn – Changing a call – Claim or concession by declarer – Claim or concession by defender – Condoning improper call or play – Defective trick – Double or redouble out of turn – Draw for partners – Dummy's rights – Exposed card – Exposed hand – Improper call – Improper remark – Inadmissible double or redouble – Inspection of tricks – Insufficient bid – Lead out of turn – Missing card – Pass out of turn – Penalty card – Penalty satisfied or forfeited – Played card – Premature lead or play – Quitted trick – Redeal – Review of bidding – Revoke corrected – Revoke established – Simultaneous call – Simultaneous lead or play – Surplus card – Unauthorized information during bidding – Unauthorized information during play.

11. Tournament procedure

Alert procedure – American whist movement – Bidding boxes – Board-a-match scoring – Bridgerama – Butler method – [see below] Convention card – Conventions in tournament play – Duplicate scoring – Howell movement – Individual tournament – International match points – Laws of bridge – Match play – Mitchell movement – Pairs contest – Screens – Skip bid – Swiss movement – Tournament bridge – Vu-graph.

12. Definitions

Chicago – Ethics – Goulash – Master Points – Par contest – Proprieties – Scoring – Yarborough.

Cross-references

Where further information can be found in another entry, its title appears in italic type. Thus '*Astro*' or 'See *Blackwood*'.

Part 1

BIDDING

ACE-SHOWING RESPONSES TO 2 ♣

By partnership arrangement the responder to an opening 2 ♣ may show his aces immediately. With no aces he bids 2 ◇. With one ace he bids the suit in which the ace is held (3 ◇ to show the ace of diamonds). With two aces he bids 3 NT. An alternative scheme is to respond 2 NT with two aces, 3 NT with fair values such as three kings but no ace. In response to a subsequent *Blackwood* 4 NT, responder can show his kings.

The idea is attributed to the former French champion, the late Pierre Albarran. Ace-showing responses to 2 ♣ are a feature of the *CAB System*.

ACOL SYSTEM

This is the standard British system of bidding, popular also in many European countries. It is a natural system in which most bids mean what they say. It has more limit bids and sign-offs than Standard American. The main features are:

1. Opening suit bids of one are in the range of 13 to 20 points. Opening 1 NT is variable: 12 to 14 not vulnerable, 15 to 17 vulnerable.

2. The opening 2 ♣ suggests 23 points or more in a balanced hand; with distribution and five quick tricks there may be no more than 19.

3. Opening bids of 2 ◇, 2 ♡ or 2 ♠, known as Acol two-bids, are forcing for one round. If a one-suiter, the hand should contain about eight playing tricks or more. A powerful two-suiter such as ♠x ♡A K J 9 x x ◇A K J x x ♣x also qualifies. The usual range for this type is about 16 to 19 points. The negative response is traditionally 2 NT, but an alternative is to respond in the next suit (see *Herbert Convention*) on weakness and to bid 2 NT to show positive values in the relay suit (e.g. 2 NT over 2 ♡ would be a positive in spades, 2 NT over 2 ♠ a positive in clubs).

4. Raises of partner's suit and notrump responses are limit bids. Thus, in response to an opening 1 ♠, a raise to 3 ♠ suggests about 10 to 12 points, including distribution, a response of 2 NT about 11 to 12 points in high cards.

The *Stayman Convention* is part of the system, and among tournament players many other conventions are common, such as

Blackwood, Flint, Fourth Suit Forcing, Transfer Bids, Unusual No-trump.

Historically, Acol began as a distinctive British system, breaking away from some of Ely Culbertson's more rigid notions. The system was first played at a club in Acol Road, Hampstead, in 1934. The philosophy of the early days was summed up in the saying, 'You bid what you think you can make and you pass when you feel like it.' Another aphorism was that Acol was not so much a system of bidding as an attitude of mind. Among modern tournament players Acol has lost much of its free-wheeling style.

ADVANCE CUE BID

It is normal to agree a trump suit before embarking on cue bids that show controls, but sometimes there is not room to do this. On such occasions a player may make an advance cue bid before directly expressing support. For example:

Opener	Responder
1 ♠	2 ♢
3 ♠	?

Responder holds:

♠K 10 9   ♡Q 4   ♢K Q 9 8 3   ♣A 5 4

A raise to 4 ♠ would be inadequate and a jump to 5 ♠ would not identify the controls. The best move for the moment is a cue bid of 4 ♣. Later, support for spades (e.g. 5 ♠ over 4 ♢ or 5 ♣) will clarify the position.

In the example above, responder's 4 ♣ is ambiguous in that it may theoretically be based on a minor two-suiter, but in many cases the logic of the sequence will proclaim an advance cue bid.

Opener	Responder
1 NT	3 ♠
4 ♢	

Opener indicates better than average support for spades and at the same time a diamond control. With a less promising hand he would simply raise to 4 ♠ or bid 3 NT.

ADVANCE SACRIFICE

When a player is prepared to sacrifice at a certain level, it may be good tactics for him to bid at that level before he has to. This is called an advance sacrifice or advance save. The intention is to crowd the auction and present the opponents with a difficult decision. For example, with North-South vulnerable the bidding goes:

South	West	North	East
1 ♢	1 ♡	2 ♠	5 ♡

East holds:

♠85   ♡QJ942   ♢Q8743   ♣9

East is prepared to go to 5 ♡ and his jump deprives opponents of the opportunity to exchange information—for example, by use of *Blackwood*.

ASKING BIDS

Asking bids are a conventional way of locating specific controls for slam purposes. They were developed in the 1930s by Ely Culbertson and his team of advisers. They have fallen out of fashion in America but are popular in some European countries and provide the basis for the special asking bids in such systems as *Precision*.

In the original scheme a bid is an Ask when it is either:
(*a*) A bid in a new suit at the four level or higher, following immediately upon the agreement of a trump suit; or
(*b*) an unnecessary jump in a new suit at the level of three or higher. The Ask will then be one level higher than a normal forcing bid. Examples:

South	North
1 ♠	3 ♠
4 ♢ (asking bid)	

South	North
1 ♣	3 ♣
4 ♠ (asking bid)	

South	North
1 ♢	3 ♠ (asking bid)

South	North
1 ♠	2 ♣
4 ♣	4 ♠ (not an asking bid)

The response to an asking bid depends on the controls held in the 'asked' suit and the controls held in other suits. Controls are defined as follows:

First-round control—ace or void
Second-round control—king or singleton
Third-round control—queen or doubleton

Responses to the first asking bid

Controls in asked suit	Controls in other suits	Response
No first- or second-round	Immaterial	Sign off in agreed trump suit
Second-round	No first-round	Sign off in agreed trump suit
Second-round	One first-round	Bid the first-round control. (With trump ace, jump one step.)
First-round	No first-round	Raise asked suit
Second-round	Two aces	Bid 4 NT
Ace	One ace	Bid 4 NT
Second-round	Three aces	Bid 5 NT
Ace	Two aces	Bid 5 NT

Where the responder has the requirements for a 4 NT response and a void in an outside suit, he may jump in the suit of the void.

There are also ways of making repeat asking bids in the same suit or subsequent asking bids in another suit.

It is assumed in the above table that the asking bid was made at the four level. If it was made at another level the responses vary accordingly.

Asking bids may be used in conjunction with a 4 NT convention such as *Blackwood*. In different forms they are included in many continental systems.

ASTRO

This is a method of competing against an opponent's 1 NT opening, using conventional overcalls of 2 ♣ and 2 ◇. The name is derived from the initial letters of the inventors, Allinger, Stern and Rosler. It may be used by either the second hand or by the fourth hand. After 1 NT:

2 ♣ shows hearts and a minor suit
2 ◇ shows spades and *another* suit

An Astro overcall suggests at least nine cards in the two suits. The following is the sort of hand with which second hand, not vulnerable, might overcall a strong 1 NT in a pairs contest:

♠ 8 3   ♡ K Q 10 8   ◇ A Q J 7 5   ♣ J 2

This hand is not strong enough for a double and a bid of 2 ◇ would place all the eggs in one basket. The Astro overcall of 2 ♣, showing hearts and a minor suit, is a reasonable speculation.

The responder to Astro proceeds as follows:
1. With three-card or longer support for the 'anchor' major, he bids this suit at an appropriate level. Thus a response of 2 ♡ in the above example would show no game ambitions, and a bid of 3 ♡ would be a game invitation with at least four-card support.
2. With a good hand he bids 2 NT, forcing for one round but not guaranteeing a further bid. This call suggests some support for the anchor major.
3. With length in the artificial suit he may pass or even raise.
4. With an independent six-card suit of his own he may bid that suit.
5. Lacking any of these features, he bids the intermediate suit, 2 ◇ in the above example. The Astro bidder will normally pass if this relay strikes his own suit, as it would in the example above.

Some partnerships extend the Astro idea. A variation called Pin-Point Astro identifies the two-suiter as follows:

2 ♣ shows hearts and clubs
2 ◇ shows hearts and diamonds
2 ♡ shows hearts and spades
2 ♠ shows spades and a minor suit

See also *Brozel, Cansino, Landy, Ripstra*, and *Sharples Defence to 1 NT*.

ASTRO CUE BID

Immediate overcalls in the opponent's suit are underemployed in standard systems. Hands on which the defender hopes to make game even if partner is weak occur rarely, and when they do they can be introduced with a take-out double. A suggestion from the authors of the Astro Convention is that the immediate cue bid be used to show two-suited hands that include one major suit and one minor suit.

1 ♣–2 ♣ shows hearts and diamonds
1 ◇–2 ◇ shows hearts and clubs
1 ♡–2 ♡ shows spades and clubs
1 ♠–2 ♠ shows hearts and clubs

In effect, the cue bid shows the lower unbid major suit and the lower unbid minor suit. The major suit will often be of four cards and the minor suit longer. Such hands are difficult to introduce by standard methods.

When not vulnerable, the cue bid is mainly defensive in purpose. Vulnerable, the strength will be equal to a sound vulnerable overcall in the minor suit, with the added information of length in a major.

♠9   ♡AJ742   ◇6   ♣QJ10842

Not vulnerable, overcall 1 ♠ with 2 ♠.

♠5   ♡AQ104   ◇AQJ962   ♣53

Vulnerable, overcall 1 ♣ with 2 ♣.
Compare *Michaels Cue Bid*.

BALANCING

When the opponents have opened the bidding and have allowed it to die at a low level, a player may be justified in reopening on a moderate hand in the expectation that his partner holds fair values. This is called a 'balancing' or 'protective' bid. A common example is where an opening suit bid of one is passed round to the fourth hand:

South	West	North	East
1 ♡	Pass	Pass	?

Any simple bid in East's position promises less than if made by the second hand. The theory is that North must be very weak to pass his partner's opening, and West may have passed with a useful hand that was not well suited to immediate action. The normal range for a simple suit bid by East in this position is about 8–13 points in high cards; a bid of 1 NT suggests 11 to 14 points. 1 NT is often the best move on balanced hands even when no guard is held in opener's suit. In general, 1 NT over a minor tends to be stronger than over a major, because there is more room for a simple suit call.

A take-out double, too, may be made on less than is required in second position. The following would be sufficient for double of 1 ♡ at equal vulnerability:

♠K 10 7 4   ♡3   ◇A 10 4   ♣Q 9 8 3 2

A double in the balancing position is passed for penalties more often than a double in second position. Fourth hand should therefore not double on defenceless hands; a void in the opponent's suit is a distinct handicap.

Balancing on the second round

Good players—at duplicate and match play, especially—dislike letting opponents play at a contract of their own choice at the level of one or two. It is therefore common to reopen on the second round on quite moderate values when it is clear that both opponents are limited.

South	West	North	East
1 ◇	Pass	1 ♡	Pass
2 ♡	Pass	Pass	?

East holds:

♠Q 9 5 4   ♡7 3   ◇A J 7   ♣K 10 4 2

It would be aggressive, but by no means unreasonable, to contest with a double. An important element in this borderline decision is that opponents have found a mild fit in hearts. This makes it safer to contest, as East-West are more likely now to find a fit of their own. Suppose instead that the bidding had been:

South	West	North	East
1 ◇	Pass	1 ♡	Pass
2 ◇	Pass	Pass	?

It would now be unsound for East to reopen. North may quite possibly hold about a 10-point 4–4–1–4 type and be ready to slaughter any competition by his opponents.

BARON GRAND SLAM TRY

This is a convention for locating top cards in the trump suit, proposed in the *Baron System* and still used by many good players. It allows more scope for judgement than the *Grand Slam Force*.

When a trump suit has been agreed, a bid of six in the suit below the agreed trump suit is a grand slam try. It asks the responder to call the grand slam if his trumps are 'good'. The responder has to exercise his judgement, deciding whether or not his trumps are better than his previous bidding has suggested. For example, West holds:

♠A Q 9 7 4 3   ♡A 10 5   ◇K J 7   ♣3

The bidding goes:

West	East
1 ♠	2 ◇
3 ◇	4 ♠
4 NT	5 ♡ (two aces)
6 ♡	

West's 6 ♡ requests his partner to bid seven if he holds fair trumps. East will now place particular value on the king of spades, if he holds this card.

BARON SYSTEM

This British system, developed in the 1940s primarily by Leo Baron and Adam Meredith, no longer has a large following, but many of the ideas it introduced are to be found in modern systems, notably the *Weak Notrump* throughout (12½ to 13½ originally), *Baron 2 NT Response*, *Baron Grand Slam Try*, *Fourth Suit Forcing*, *Inverted Minor Suit Raises*, and Baron over 2 NT where 3 ♣ asks for four-card suits to be shown 'upwards' (see *Two Notrump Opening*). Less popular, but not unknown, are such arrangements as simple change of suit forcing, all four-card suits biddable, a 1 NT overcall equivalent to a weak take-out double. The only Baron idea that has been universally discarded is that of making all simple overcalls strong, equal to an opening bid.

BARON 2 NT RESPONSE

In the *Baron System* a direct response of 2 NT to an opening of one of a suit is forcing, showing a balanced 16–18 points (or the range may be 15–19). This feature has been adopted by exponents of some other systems. A hand of this strength is otherwise difficult to describe.

Over the 2 NT response, opener bids his hand naturally.

BENJAMIN CONVENTION

Originated by the Scottish player, Albert Benjamin, this convention proposes a scheme that includes both weak and strong two-bids. It is popular with *Acol* players and can be used with any approach-forcing system, replacing the two-bids normally used.

Opening bid of 2 ♣. This is the opening on any hand strong enough for a one-round force, regardless of which is the long suit. The negative response is 2 ◊. Any other response is game-forcing. The method makes possible an Acol two-bid in clubs.

Opening bid of 2 ◊. This is equivalent to an Acol 2 ♣ opening and is forcing to game except when the rebid is 2 NT. The negative response is 2 ♡.

Opening bid of 2 ♡ *or 2* ♠. These are weak two-bids, showing 6–11 points and a six-card suit.

An opening bid of 2 ♣ or 2 ◊ followed by a rebid in notrumps shows a strong, balanced hand. The scheme proposed by the author of the convention is as follows:

2 NT opening shows 19–20 points

2 ♣–2 ◊–2 NT	21–22
2 ◊–2 ♡–2 NT	23–24
2 ♣–2 ◊–3 NT	25–26
2 ◊–2 ♡–3 NT	27–28

BIDDABLE SUITS

Only beginners use defined standards for biddable suits. Most players, however, unless they employ a system such as *Blue Club*, avoid opening a weak four-card major suit, preferring instead a three-card minor or 1 NT.

On the second round more or less any four-card suit is admissible when there is no better choice, but there are some situations where practice differs. For example:

South	North
1 ♣	1 ♡
?	

South holds:

♠9843　♡Q5　◇KJ2　♣AQJ3

Some players would rebid 1 ♠, others 1 NT; it is as much a matter of style as of system. There tends to be more general agreement about the next situation:

South	North
1 ♠	2 ♣
2 ♡	

South holds:

♠AQJ52　♡J983　◇Q10　♣A8

Most players would be willing to introduce the moderate heart suit. A bid of 2 ♠ in this sequence may be preferred with 6–4 in the major suits, but seldom with 5–4.

The situation changes when a slam may be in the offing. It is then inadvisable to bid weak suits, so if the bidding began 1 ♠–3 ♣ opener would be more likely to rebid 3 ♠ with the above hand.

Some systems, including *Precision*, require five cards for an opening 1 ♡ or 1 ♠. In North America, many 'standard' players employ this rule too, especially in first or second position. See *Five-card Majors*.

BLACKWOOD CONVENTION

Invented by Easley Blackwood in 1933, this convention has since enjoyed world-wide popularity. To find out how many aces his partner holds, a player bids 4 NT. In reply, his partner shows his total number of aces in accordance with a step system:

5 ♣ shows no ace or four	5 ♡ shows two aces
5 ◇ shows one ace	5 ♠ shows three aces

If the 4 NT bidder calls 5 NT over his partner's response, he announces that all four aces are held in the combined hands and asks partner to show kings in the same way.

Void suits

These are not counted as aces when responding to Blackwood, but there are several ways in which voids can be shown. In the method recommended by Blackwood himself, the responder to 4 NT bids the suit that shows the appropriate number of aces, but he bids it at the six level. For example, with two aces and a void he would respond 6 ♡ instead of 5 ♡. This action is taken only when the general strength of the hand warrants the high-level response and when the void is in a suit that partner is likely to be able to identify. In some cases a player with one ace and a void, if confident that the void will be useful, may respond at the six level, but not going beyond the level of the agreed suit.

5 NT to play

When the Blackwood bidder, on hearing the ace-showing response, wishes to stop short of slam, he may be able to call a halt in 5 NT. He cannot call 5 NT direct, as that would ask for kings. Instead, he calls five in any unbid suit. This requires partner to call 5 NT, which can be passed.

In general, the Blackwood convention is used only when it has already been established that enough tricks for slam are present. It should be regarded as insurance against reaching a slam when two aces are missing. 4 NT is correct when all a player wants to know is how many aces partner holds (and when a disappointing reply will not endanger game). It is usually incorrect when a player has two losers in an unbid suit or has a void suit.

When opponents intervene

The responder to Blackwood is not obliged to show his aces if the opponents intervene over 4 NT, but he may do so if he has no reason to be ashamed of his previous bidding. He then responds by steps, starting from the opponent's bid. For example:

South	*West*	*North*	*East*
1 ♡	Pass	3 ♡	4 ◇
4 NT	5 ◇	?	

If North bids 5 ♡, this shows one ace. 5 ♠ would promise two aces, and so on. A pass would mean either that North had no ace or that he was not prepared to show one. A double would be for penalties.

There are, however, several conventions that use a double in this situation as part of a scheme of ace-showing bids. The most widely used are those known by the mnemonics, DEPO, DOPI and PODI:

DEPO means Double Even, Pass Odd. Thus a double shows 0, 2 or 4 aces, a pass shows 1 or 3.

DOPI means Double 0, Pass 1. Two or more aces are shown by steps: thus, over an interference of 5 ♡, a bid of 5 ♠ shows two aces.

PODI means Pass 0, Double 1. Here the DOPI scheme is reversed, but two or more aces are still shown by steps.

For sequences where 4 NT is not Blackwood but natural, see *Quantitative 4 NT*. For variations, see *Byzantine Blackwood, Four-Club Blackwood, Five-ace Blackwood, Gerber Convention*, and *Roman Blackwood*.

BLUE CLUB SYSTEM

This Italian system is closely related to the Neapolitan Club. Its chief features are:

1 ♣ opening is forcing and normally shows at least 17 points, 18 on a balanced hand. Responses show controls by steps, counting an ace as two controls and a king as one. 1 ◇ shows 0–2 controls, less than 6 points; 1 ♡ shows 0–2 controls, 6+ points; 1 ♠ shows three controls, and so on up to 2 ◇.

1 ◇, 1 ♡, and 1 ♠ openings are natural and limited, showing 12–16 points and at least a four-card suit. With two suits of unequal length, the shorter is bid first unless the hand is a minimum and the longer suit is higher ranking. Most responses are normal.

1 NT opening shows a balanced hand with either 13–15 points and a club suit, or 16–17 points.

2 ♣ opening shows 12–16 points with at least a good five-card club suit. If a second suit is held, opener will usually have 15 or 16 points.

2 ◇ opening shows a powerful three-suited hand with 17–24 points.

2 ♡ and 2 ♠ openings are normal weak two-bids.

Defensive bidding is normal, but overcalls are made freely.

BROZEL

This system of defence against an opponent's 1 NT opening enables the overcaller to indicate (*a*) that he has an unspecified long suit; or (*b*) that he has a particular two-suiter; or (*c*) that he has a fairly strong three-suiter. This is the scheme:

(*a*) A double of 1 NT (either in second or fourth position) shows the values for a normal one-suited overcall. Partner may decide to pass for penalties; otherwise, he will bid 2 ♣ and allow the doubler to name his suit.

(*b*) Overcalls at the two-level indicate two-suiters according to the following schedule:

2 NT shows the minors.
2 ♠ shows spades and a minor.
2 ♡ shows hearts and spades.
2 ♢ shows diamonds and hearts.
2 ♣ shows hearts and clubs.

(*c*) A jump overcall is an *Exclusion Bid*, denoting a pronounced three-suiter, probably 5–4–4–0, with a shortage in the suit named.

See, also, the defensive systems listed under *Astro*.

BYZANTINE BLACKWOOD

Devised mainly by Jack Marx, of London, this 4 NT convention is based on the idea of including 'key-suit' kings as well as aces. Key suits include the trump suit, any genuine side suit that has been bid and supported, and any suit bid by a player whose partner's first bid was in notrumps. The convention is abandoned when there are more than two key suits. But if there is only one key suit, a king of a 'half-key' suit—that is, a genuine suit that has been bid but not supported—may be shown.

When there is only one key suit the Byzantine responses to 4 NT are:

5 ♣ no ace, or three aces, or two aces plus the key-suit king.
5 ♢ one ace, or four aces, or three aces plus the key-suit king.
5 ♡ two aces, or the A K Q of the key suit, or the A K of the key suit plus the king of the half-key suit.
5 ♠ two aces plus the K Q of the key suit, or three aces plus the king of the half-key suit.
5 NT three aces plus the K Q of the key suit, or all the aces plus the king of the key suit.

When there are two key suits, half-key kings are not shown. The meaning of the 5 ♣ and 5 ◇ responses is unchanged, but the higher responses are as follows:

> 5 ♡ two aces or the A K Q of a key suit, or one ace and both key-suit kings.
>
> 5 ♠ two aces plus the K Q of a key suit, or two aces and both key-suit kings, or one ace plus the king of one key suit and the K Q of the other key suit.
>
> 5 NT three aces plus the K Q of a key suit, or three aces and both key-suit kings, or all the aces plus one key-suit king, or two aces plus the king of one key suit and the K Q of the other, or one ace and the K Q of both key suits.

CAB SYSTEM

This British system has lost in popularity since the death of some of its leading exponents, notably Leslie Dodds and Kenneth Konstam. The initials CAB stand for two Clubs, Ace responses, Blackwood.

In general style, CAB resembles Standard American rather than Acol. A response of 2 NT to an opening bid of one is forcing, and so is a double raise of a suit opening. An opening 1 NT is strong throughout and a take-out into two of a suit is forcing. A response at the two level to a suit bid of one promises 10 points and a rebid of 2 NT by the opener signifies a minimum.

CANAPÉ

The term describes a style of bidding in which the shorter of two biddable suits is called before the longer. For example:

♠ A Q 10 x x   ♡ K Q J x   ◇ x x   ♣ K x

The opening bid on this hand is 1 ♡. When spades are shown on the next round, partner knows that the spades are longer than the hearts. In such a sequence the opener will have imparted more information than in a standard sequence. Moreover, as a preference to the first suit is unlikely, the partnership will be able to stay at a safe level on most minimum hands. The same principle applies when the shorter suit is the higher ranking. Thus, when an opening bid of 1 ♠ is followed by 2 ♡ on the second round, this shows that the hearts are at least as long as the spades and may be longer.

The Canapé method, as opposed to *la longue d'abord* (long suit first), is popular in France and an important feature of some of the Italian systems, such as the *Blue Club* and *Roman System*.

A Canapé sequence is not necessarily followed on minimum hands. Four-card major suits are usually bid ahead of any minor suit.

CANSINO DEFENCE

This is one of the most flexible systems of defence against an opponent's 1 NT opening. An overall of 2 ♣ shows a limited hand, not strong enough for a double, with clubs and two other suits. It guarantees a singleton. With no game ambitions responder may pass 2 ♣ or bid his lowest-ranking suit, the bidding dying as soon as a fit is found.

An overcall of 2 ◇ shows in principle short clubs and values in the other suits. The overcall is also reasonably safe with a major two-suiter. These conventional overcalls have the same sense in both second and fourth position.

Over 2 ♣ a response of 2 NT is forcing. The 2 ♣ bidder then calls 3 ♣ to show a singleton heart, 3 ◇ to show a singleton spade, and 3 NT to show a singleton diamond. A bid of three of a major promises a five-card suit.

Over 2 ◇ the forcing response is 3 ◇. Other responses are limited.

There is an additional arrangement: since it is seldom profitable to double a strong notrump, and since a player who has passed cannot have a sound double of 1 NT, a double in these circumstances indicates either a major or minor two-suiter.

See, also, the defensive systems listed under *Astro*.

CARROT CLUB

This Swedish system resembles the *Blue Club* in general structure, but has specialized responses to the 1 ♣ opening (17 points upwards). These are: 1 ◇, 0–7; 1 ♡, 8 or more, denies a 5-card major, 6-card minor, or 5–5 in the minors (which are expressed by separate responses); 1 ♠, 8 or more with five hearts; 1 NT, 8 or more with five spades; 2 ♣ and 2 ◇, six-card minor or 5–5 in the minors; 2 NT, any solid suit; suit at three level, K Q J x x x. All relay bids over these responses are artificial.

Opening bids of one in other suits are natural, 11–16. 1 NT may be 13 or 14 with no major, or any 15–17 balanced. Opening 2 ♣ is 11–16, natural, 2 ◇ is *Multicoloured*, 2 ♡ and 2 ♠ show the major suit and clubs, 2 NT a minor two-suiter.

COMIC NOTRUMP

See *Gardener Notrump Overcall*.

COMPETITIVE DOUBLES

When both sides are bidding freely at a low level, the opportunity for a penalty double does not often arise. Among tournament players there is a strong tendency to use the double as 'competitive', indicating that the doubler does not wish to bow out at this stage but has no satisfactory natural call to make. In *Bridge for Tournament Players* the present authors propose this scheme:

Competitive doubles by the opening side

1. When both sides have found a fit, a double by the opening side up to the level of three is competitive when there is no room for any other game try. This provides a solution to a frequent problem.

South	West	North	East
1 ♠	2 ♡	2 ♠	3 ♡
?			

Playing the competitive double, a double here is not for penalties but says: 'If you are not minimum we have a good chance to make 4 ♠.' In the US this double would be called a 'maximal overcall double'. A bid of 3 ♠, ambiguous in standard methods, is now purely competitive and not a game try. If the opponents had been bidding clubs, however, South would have room for a trial bid of 3 ◇ or 3 ♡ and in this case a double would be for penalties.

2. When only the defending side has found a fit, a double by the opening side is competitive up to the level of two. (When the opening side has not so far found a fit, a double at the three level is more likely to be needed as a penalty measure.)

3. At the two level or below, the competitive double tends to show that no sound alternative is available:

South	West	North	East
1 ♣	1 ♡	1 ♠	2 ♡
Double			

This says: 'I have no good bid available but we can do better than let them play in 2 ♡.'

Competitive doubles by the defending side

Defenders have even less use than the opening side for penalty doubles at a low level.

South	West	North	East
1 ♡	1 ♠	2 ◇	?

East will seldom want to double for penalties at this point, for the sequence is forcing. East might hold:

♠ 10 4   ♡ A 8 2   ◇ K 7 5   ♣ K 6 5 3 2

This is the general scheme for competitive doubles by the defending side:

1. When the opening side has bid two suits, a double at the level of one or two is competitive when only one member of the side has so far entered the bidding. It suggests tolerance, but not primary support, for partner's suit; length in the unbid suit; and ability to contest.

2. When the opening side has bid only one suit, the doubler may hold either length in both unbid suits together with bare tolerance for partner's suit, or length in one of the unbid suits and moderate support for partner's suit.

CONTROLS

First-round control of a suit means the ace or, in a suit contract, a void in the suit. Second-round control means the guarded king, or a singleton in a suit contract.

The following conventions are designed primarily for the location of controls in slam bidding and are listed under their respective titles: *Asking Bids, Blackwood Convention, Byzantine Blackwood, Culbertson Four-Five Notrump, Declarative-Interrogative (DI) 4 NT, Five-ace Blackwood, Gerber Convention* and *Roman Blackwood.*

Controls may also be identified by cue-bidding, which can be used in addition to a 4 NT convention.

For controls in connection with psychic bidding, see *Psychic Controls*.

CONVENTIONS

A convention is a partnership arrangement whereby a special meaning, not obvious to the opponents, is attached to a bid or play. Some conventions, such as the take-out double or the echo to show a doubleton, are more or less universal. Many others, such as *Stayman*, are so well known that except in a beginner's game it is not necessary to do more than state that the convention is played.

Conventions become a matter for controversy when they are intricate or when they confront an opponent with an unfamiliar problem. Thus a convention such as the *Multicoloured 2 ◇*, if employed in a pairs tournament, may present opponents with a tactical problem against which they have prepared no counter-measures.

Consequently, in most clubs and duplicate circles it is usual to restrict the use of conventions to those that are generally known to the other players. In the tournament world most ruling bodies require competitors to be furnished with a 'convention card' showing the partnership's basic bidding and play agreements. In addition, there is provision for 'alerting' the opponents to the fact that a particular bid has a conventional meaning.

In most countries inventors of new systems and conventions have to obtain a licence from the ruling body before their brain-child can be used. In North America the American Contract Bridge League places licensed conventions in one of six classes, ranging from Class A, which the Tournament Committee *must* allow to be played in all local or higher rated events, to Class F, which may be authorized for use only in matches of 16 boards or more.

Departures from conventions

It is never unethical for a player to depart from a convention that he has announced, provided that partner is not in on the secret.

CO-OPERATIVE DOUBLE

There are many situations where a player makes a double that is, by definition, a penalty double, but does not expect partner to pass unless the double suits him well. A double of that kind is said to be co-operative. For example:

(1)	*South*	*West*	*North*	*East*
	1 ◇	Pass	1 NT	2 ♣
	2 ◇	3 ♣	Pass	Pass
	Double			

(2)	*South*	*West*	*North*	*East*
	1 ♡	2 ♣	2 ♡	3 ♣
	Pass	Pass	Double	

Clearly the doubler intends that partner should use his discretion in deciding whether to pass or to bid three of the suit. In each case the doubler has described his hand within reasonable limits, notably in failing to double on the previous round.

The co-operative double, which arises from the logic of the situation, should be distinguished from the conventional manoeuvres, *Competitive Double, Negative Double, Optional Double* and *Responsive Double.*

CROWHURST CONVENTION

In standard bidding a rebid of 1 NT by a player who has opened with a bid of one has a narrow range; depending on whether the opening 1 NT is weak or strong, the rebid is 15–16 or 12–14 points. The Crowhurst convention enables the 1 NT rebid to be made with a hand in the 12–16 point range, without loss of accuracy. Playing Crowhurst, a bid of 2 ♣ by responder on the second round is conventional after the opener has rebid 1 NT. For example:

South	*North*
1 ◇	1 ♠
1 NT	2 ♣

In this sequence the 1 NT rebid shows 12–16 points. Responder may raise to 3 NT with 13 points or more and he may make an invitational raise to 2 NT if he has 11 points or a poor 12. When responder has 10 points, or a promising 9, he bids 2 ♣, to see whether opener is maximum.

Opener's rebids over 2 ♣ are as follows:
1. With 15 or 16 points, opener rebids 2 NT.
2. With 12–14 points, opener may:
   (*a*) Show three-card support for responder's major suit.
   (*b*) Rebid a five-card heart suit.
   (*c*) Show a four-card heart suit which previously had been concealed.
   (*d*) Failing any of these alternatives, bid 2 ◇.
Crowhurst is popular with British tournament players, one advantage being that opener can choose more freely between one of a suit and 1 NT. There is a modification, called the 'impossible major'. If, in response to a 2 ♣ enquiry, opener introduces a major suit not previously bid by the partnership, he shows a poor to average 15 points. This enables the bidding to be halted at 2 NT when responder has only 9 points.

CUE BID BY OPENING SIDE

When used by the opening side the traditional sense of a cue bid in opponent's suit was to confirm partner's suit and express good values. The bid can still be used in that sense but more often it is a general-purpose bid with the meaning: 'We have enough combined strength to advance, but I am not sure in which direction.'

South	*West*	*North*	*East*
1 ♠	Pass	2 ♣	2 ◇
3 ◇			

North-South are vulnerable and South holds:

♠ A J 10 9 3   ♡ A K 5   ◇ 10 9 5   ♣ A 8

After North's two-level response South does not want to fall short of game. The cue bid of 3 ◇ is a general-purpose force which says nothing about South's holding in diamonds. There is an inference that South lacks an independent guard, as then he might have bid notrumps.

The cue bid may be used in this sense whenever game values are present. North opens 1 ♣, East overcalls with 1 ♠, and South holds:

♠ 9 8 2   ♡ A 8 7 4   ◇ K J 2   ♣ A Q 8

A cue bid of 2 ♠ is a sound move (but see also *Negative Double*).

CUE-BID OVERCALL

In standard bidding the strongest way to enter the auction, some-times called a 'direct cue bid', is an immediate cue bid of a suit that the opponents have already bid:

South	West	North	East
Pass	Pass	1 ♡	2 ♡

East's 2 ♡ used to be played as unconditionally forcing to game. By partnership arrangement, however, the bidding may be dropped when one player has shown minimum preference for his partner's suit or when the strong hand has supported a forced call. For example:

South	West	North	East
Pass	Pass	1 ♡	2 ♡
Pass	2 ♠	Pass	3 ♠

West may pass with a worthless hand, for East could have raised straight to game.

The cue bid does not guarantee first-round control in the oppo-nents' suit.

When the opponents have called two suits it is usual to play that a game-forcing overcall may be made only in the suit last bid:

South	West	North	East
1 ♣	Pass	1 ♠	2 ♣

East's 2 ♣ is not a cue-bid overcall. It promises a suit that is playable despite the bid on the left. (An alternative scheme is to treat 2 ♣ in that sequence as a less powerful overcall than 2 ♠.)

For specialized uses of the cue-bid overcall, see *Astro Cue Bids* and *Michaels Cue Bids*. For the meaning of cue bids at other stages of the auction, see *Cue Bid by Opening Side*, and *Cue Bid to Show Controls*.

CUE BID TO SHOW CONTROLS

In a constructive, uncontested, auction the term cue bid has the specific meaning of a control-showing bid. A cue bid in this sense can be made only when a trump suit has been agreed expressly or by inference, and the bid generally amounts to a slam suggestion.

The level at which the cue bid is made must be such that the partnership is committed to game at least. Thus in the following auction 4 ♣ is a cue bid:

South	North
1 ◇	1 ♠
3 ♠	4 ♣

Over 3 ♠ any call commits the partnership to game, so 4 ♣ must be a slam suggestion.

In the next auction 3 ♣ is *not* a cue bid, because the partnership is not committed to game:

South	North
1 ♡	2 ♡
3 ♣	

3 ♣ is merely a try for game. (See *Trial Bid*.)

When a player has more than one control he usually cue-bids the one that can be shown at the lowest level.

A cue bid does not demand a conventional response. The responder is free to judge whether to sign off, cue-bid in his turn, or take other strong action.

Cue bids to show second-round controls

When first-round control of a suit has been shown by a cue bid, a subsequent cue bid in that suit by either player shows second-round control. Thus:

South	North
1 ♡	3 ♡
3 ♠	4 ♣
5 ♣	

Here South is showing second-round control of clubs and there is a clear inference that he does not have first-round control of diamonds.

When no other convenient slam try is available, a player—and especially the subordinate partner—may cue-bid the second-round control of a suit when first-round control has not been shown. The bidding goes:

South	North
1 ♠	3 ♠
4 ♣	?

North has an opportunity to indicate either first- or second-round control of either red suit.

See also *Advance Cue Bid*.

CULBERTSON 4–5 NT

Introduced as part of the Culbertson system in the early 1930s, this was the first convention to attach a special meaning to a bid of 4 NT. It differs from *Blackwood* in that it gives, as well as seeks, information. Also, there is more latitude for the exercise of judgement in selecting the response to 4 NT. Less simple than Blackwood, the convention has few adherents today.

Qualifications for 4 NT

A conventional bid of 4 NT guarantees three aces, or two aces and a king of a genuine suit bid by the partnership.

Responses to 4 NT

1. Lacking an ace, or the kings of all bid suits, responder signs off by calling five in the lowest genuine suit that has been bid by either partner.
2. With an ace or a void of an unbid suit, he bids five in that suit. But he has the option of signing off instead if his judgement tells him that a brake should be applied (notably when the control is in a suit of higher rank than the agreed trump suit).
3. With an ace of a bid suit, or with the kings of all bid suits, he bids six in the agreed trump suit, or five of a suit which is not the lowest valued. But again he may use his judgement and sign off instead.
4. With two aces, or one ace and the kings of all the bid suits, he bids 5 NT.

4 NT followed by 5 NT

A player who holds the four aces can show them by calling 4 NT and following with 5 NT after partner has signed off.

CULBERTSON SYSTEM

The 'approach forcing' methods developed by Ely Culbertson and published in his *Blue Book* (1933) and *Gold Book* (1936) became standard practice in many countries until the early 1950s. The Culbertson System as such is now little played, although American standard bidding is not much different.

Culbertson introduced many special conventions which may be used independently of his system. See *Asking Bids, Culbertson Four-five Notrump* and *Trump Asking Bids*.

DECLARATIVE-INTERROGATIVE 4 NT

Italian systems such as the *Blue Club* make limited use of conventional *Blackwood*. When not a jump, and when not bid on the first or second round, 4 NT is a general slam try, bearing the cumbersome title above. The responder may sign off in the agreed trump suit; if not so doing, he shows extra controls or additional length.

DEFENCE TO 1 ♣ BIDS

When the modern 1 ♣ bids became widely popular, defenders formed plans to enter the auction as soon as possible to interfere with the exchange of information after a conventional opening. Since there is seldom good reason for bidding a natural 1 NT over a strong 1 ♣, or for doubling for take-out with a strong hand, it became common to attach a conventional meaning to these two calls. Thus 1 NT may express a minor two-suiter, double a major two-suiter. Jump overcalls in a suit are pre-emptive and simple overcalls are natural.

Many more elaborate schemes for defence against a strong 1 ♣ have been developed. This is one system:
(*a*) A minimum call in any suit (1 ◇ up to 2 ♣) shows a two-suiter with the suit named and the one immediately above.
(*b*) 1 NT shows hearts and clubs.
(*c*) Double shows spades and diamonds.
(*d*) Any jump, such as 2 ♡, indicates a primarily one-suited hand.
(*e*) With a strong hand of any kind, second hand can pass and perhaps enter later.

The experience of the authors, gained from both sides of the fence, is that none of these schemes is particularly helpful. The notion of indicating a two-suiter, in the hope that partner will be able to jump to the skies in one suit or the other, looks better on the drawing-board than at the table. The usual consequence is that the 1 ♣ side still obtains the final contract and is assisted by the information supplied by the overcall.

Another point to bear in mind is that intervention at a low level, so far from impeding the responder to a 1 ♣ opening, provides him with two additional ways of expressing his values—a pass and a negative double.

A device which is purely obstructive and does not seek to find a fit is the 'floating spade', which means that an overcall of 1 ♠ is always suspect.

DELAYED GAME RAISE

This is one of numerous techniques to express a particular type of strong supporting hand in response to an opening 1 ♡ or 1 ♠. It signifies, in principle, the values for a raise to game, including a very fair side suit. North opens 1 ♠ and South holds:

(1) ♠A 10 6 3 ♡5 ◇64 ♣AQ8642

(2) ♠KQ85 ♡K4 ◇KQ1062 ♣73

In each case South responds in the minor suit, intending to jump to 4 ♠ on the next round. The knowledge that a fair suit is held by the responding hand sometimes makes it possible to reach a slam with limited high-card values.

In some sequences the opener's rebid will deny responder the chance to express the DGR type. For example, the sequence 1 ♡–2 ♣–2 ♡–4 ♡ does not necessarily denote the type with good trump support and a fair side suit; nor does the sequence 1 ♡–2 ♣–2 NT–4 ♡. After the limited rebid responder may be willing to settle for game. If he still wants to express the DGR, he can jump in the other minor. Thus 1 ♠–2 ◇–2 NT–4 ♣ signifies DGR—good spades and good diamonds.

DEPO

See *Blackwood Convention*.

DIRECTIONAL ASKING BID

This is an attempt to solve the problem of reaching a safe game in
notrumps when neither player has in his own hand a sure guard in
the enemy suit. Here South has a familiar problem.

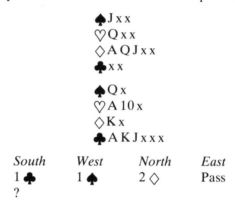

♠ J x x
♡ Q x x
◇ A Q J x x
♣ x x

♠ Q x
♡ A 10 x
◇ K x
♣ A K J x x x

South	West	North	East
1 ♣	1 ♠	2 ◇	Pass
?			

After North's diamond bid South would be willing to contract for
3 NT if he could be sure of a spade guard. Using ordinary bidding
methods, however, neither South nor North could call notrumps
with any degree of assurance, though between them they have a
sure stopper if the suit is led.

Playing directional asking bids, South rebids 2 ♠, asking North to
call notrumps if he holds a guard or a partial guard in spades. A
partial guard is Q x, or J x x, perhaps even the singleton king.

It is feasible to combine bids of this type with the more traditional
type of cue bid whereby South's 2 ♠ would indicate big support for
diamonds. With such a hand South would again bid 2 ♠ but would
indicate the type on the next round by supporting diamonds.

DISTRIBUTIONAL POINT COUNT

Various methods of valuation have been proposed in which a player
adds points for distributional features to the points counted for high
cards on the 4–3–2–1 basis. The most widely used method is known
as the *Goren* count.

For notrumps, only high-card points are counted: 4 for an ace,
3 for a king, 2 for a queen, 1 for a jack.

A player who proposes to open the bidding in a suit adds distributional points as follows: 3 for a void, 2 for each singleton, 1 for each
doubleton.

A singleton honour is reduced in value by one point unless partner bids the suit. Q J x is counted as only 2 points. A point is deducted for an aceless hand, but an extra point is added when all four aces are held.

When the responder with adequate trump support proposes to raise his partner he adds distributional points according to a different scale: 1 for a doubleton, 3 for a singleton, 5 for a void.

Responder deducts a point when he has only three trumps, or when he has a 4–3–3–3 pattern. He may 'promote' honours in partner's suit by adding a point for the king, queen or jack, but only when the trump holding does not already contain more than three points.

Partnership point-count requirements

According to the Goren count and most similar distributional counts it is reckoned that the following points are required to make game or slam:

> Game at notrumps, or in a major suit, 26.
> Game in a minor suit, 29.
> Small slam, 33.
> Grand slam, 37.

Distributional point count assists beginners to arrive at the right answer on many hands but will not improve their judgement, any more than use of a ready reckoner improves anyone's arithmetic.

DOPI

See *Blackwood Convention.*

DOUBLE RAISE OF SUIT OPENING

A double raise, one to three, may be played either as limited or as forcing. In Britain the raise is always natural and limited. In the original Culbertson and Goren systems, and still in Standard American, the double raise is forcing. This provides a convenient basis for slam exploration in certain circumstances, but it also gives rise to a grey area in the wide gap between hands suitable for a raise of 1 ♠ to 2 ♠ and those warranting a raise to 3 ♠. Thus increasingly among tournament players, even in America, the raise is 'limit', signifying usually 8 to 9 high-card points with four trumps and a singleton, up to 11 with four trumps and a doubleton.

The double raise of a minor suit, when played as 'limit', implies a hand with no biddable major. Responder would raise 1 ◇ to 3 ◇ on:

♠A5   ♡62   ◇K9864   ♣Q1083

Another style is to play the double raise of a minor as weak. See *Inverted Minor Suit Raises.*

DOUBLES

See *Competitive Doubles, Co-operative Double, Free Double, Lead-directing Doubles, Lightner Double, Negative Double, Optional Double, Penalty Double, Responsive Double and Take-out Double.*

DRURY CONVENTION

This convention is designed to solve problems sometimes encountered by a passed hand. In response to an opening 1 ♡ or 1 ♠, 2 ♣ by a passed hand is conventional, asking opener to clarify his range. If minimum or sub-minimum, opener rebids 2 ◇; if not under strength, he makes some other call. With a diamond suit it is normally safe to bid 2 ◇ and later correct the impression of a weak hand. The convention is helpful when responder has a balanced hand in the 10 to 11 point range.

Compare *SNAP.*

DUPLICATION OF VALUES

Duplication of values occurs when both players have strength in the same suit and the values overlap. An ace opposite a void, or a singleton opposite K Q J, are examples. When duplication is present, the two hands will produce fewer tricks at their best contract than would otherwise be expected.

The presence of duplication sometimes becomes apparent during the bidding, as in this example:

South	North
—	1 ◇
2 ♣	2 NT
?	

South holds:

♠K Q J   ♡A K J   ◇93   ♣Q9764

It is clear that the partnership has an abundance of high cards in the major suits, where no length is present in either hand. Rather than make any slam try, therefore, South settles for 3 NT.

Duplication of values may also exist in hand pattern. Valuation must be reassessed when both hands have a singleton in the same suit. Identical shape, such as 3–5–3–2 opposite 3–5–3–2, invariably produces a disappointing result.

EFOS

The term is derived from the initials of a system played in Sweden, called the Economical Forcing System, in which a one-over-one response to an opening bid, such as one spade in response to one heart, is simply a relay. The *Roman System* employs the same idea.

EXCLUSION BID

A swift way to express values in three suits is to bid the fourth. An example occurs in the *Roman System* after the 2 ♣ or 2 ◇ opening:

South	North
2 ◇ (3-suiter)	2 NT (forcing)
?	

Now a bid of three in any suit shows that South has a singleton or void in the suit named.

Exclusion bids have been proposed as a counter to strong 1 ♣ or 1 ◇ openings and also as a way of entering against 1 NT. It has been suggested further that a simple suit call over 1 NT should be *either* exclusion *or* a genuine suit; the responder, it is assumed, will be able to judge which is intended.

FALSE PREFERENCE

For lack of a better alternative, a player will sometimes return to partner's first suit at minimum level even when he holds greater length in the second suit. East holds:

♠ A 7 6 4 2   ♡ 9 5   ◇ J 4 3   ♣ A 8 2

The bidding proceeds:

West	East
1 ♡	1 ♠
2 ◇	?

With two aces and the jack of partner's second suit, West must keep the bidding open, and a false preference to 2 ♡ is the only sensible call.

FISHBEIN CONVENTION

This method was devised by Harry Fishbein as a defence against a pre-emptive opening by an opponent. Suppose that the opponent opens 3 ♡. An overcall of 3 ♠, the next higher-ranking suit, is used in the Fishbein convention as a request for partner to show his best suit. Partner must be very reluctant to pass, as the convention may be used on two-suited hands. In the same way, 3 ◇ is used for a take-out over 3 ♣, 3 ♡ over 3 ◇ and 4 ♣ over 3 ♠.

All other bids over an opponent's three-bid are natural. Double is for penalties and 3 NT is to play. The convention is used only by the second hand: a double by fourth hand is for take-out, as in standard practice.

The Fishbein convention can also be used against opponent's weak two-bids.

FIVE-ACE BLACKWOOD

In this variation the responder to a Blackwood 4 NT treats the king of trumps or the king of a genuine suit bid by the partnership as a 'fifth ace'. The schedule of responses then becomes: 0 or 3 aces, 5 ♣; 1 or 4 aces, 5 ◇; 2 aces and no 'good' king, 5 ♡; 2 aces and a 'good' king, 5 ♠; 2 aces and two 'good' kings, 5 NT.

The convention is as useful in a negative as in a positive sense. For example, a player who holds Q x in a suit bid by his partner may discover whether his partner has, or has not, the king of this suit in addition to the ace.

Compare *Byzantine Blackwood*.

FIVE-CARD MAJORS

Many modern systems demand, at any rate in principle, five cards for a major-suit opening. In many cases this is combined with a forcing 1 NT response.

Five-card majors bring reassurance to partner, who can raise freely with three trumps and even, in competition, with only two.

On the other hand, systems such as the *Blue Club*, where four-card majors are freely bid on minimum hands, may claim that their openings possess pre-emptive value. It is more hazardous, evidently, for opponents to contest against an opening 1 ♠ than against 1 ♣ or 1 ◇.

FLANNERY 2 ◇ (OR 2 ♡)

Hands of medium strength containing four spades and five hearts create a minor problem. If 1 ♠ is opened the partnership may end in the wrong suit, and if 1 ♡ is opened the spade suit may be 'lost'.

In the Flannery convention an opening 2 ◇ signifies a hand of 11–15 points, 4–5 in the majors. Over a response of 3 ♣ or 3 ◇ opener bids 3 NT with a fit in the minor. A response of 2 NT is forcing. With 4–5–2–2 opener rebids 3 ♡ on 11–13, 3 ♠ on 14–15, 3 NT on 14–15 and values in both minors; with three of a minor he bids the suit with three cards, with four of a minor he may jump to the four level.

It is possible to use 2 ♡ as the Flannery opening instead of 2 ◇.

FLINT CONVENTION

Devised by Jeremy Flint of London and widely adopted, this convention enables the responder to a 2 NT opening to halt the bidding in three of a major suit. The first step is to respond 3 ◇, directing the opener to bid 3 ♡. If the responder's long suit is hearts, he simply passes; and if his long suit is spades he bids 3 ♠, which the opener is expected to pass. The convention would be used on a hand like this:

♠976542   ♡43   ◇107   ♣J64

Over the forced rebid of 3 ♡ responder will transfer to 3 ♠, which the opener will normally pass. If the hearts and spades were reversed, responder would pass 3 ♡.

When the opener has an exceptionally suitable hand, he may decide nevertheless to play in a game contract. As the opener does not know at first which major his partner holds, he follows this scheme:

With strong support for hearts opener bids 3 ♠ over 3 ◇. Now if responder has hearts he goes 4 ♡ but if his suit is spades he passes. *With strong support for spades* opener bids 3 ♡, and if responder bids 3 ♠ he raises to game.

With support for both major suits opener may bid 3 NT over 3 ◇. (It is possible to devise schemes whereby the opener can be sure of becoming the declarer. For example, over 3 ◇ opener, if willing to play for game in either major, bids 4 ♣; then responder with a heart suit bids 4 ◇, and with a spade suit bids 4 ♡.)

The Flint convention does not prevent responder from developing a hand that contains a diamond suit. When the responder to 2 NT actually has diamonds he begins by bidding 3 ◇ and then continues over the conventional rebid:

South	North
2 NT	3 ◇
3 ♡	3 NT

The inference here would be that North could see slam chances in diamonds.

FLINT-PENDER

This system, devised by the Anglo-American partnership of Jeremy Flint and Peter Pender, has the following general structure: weak notrump throughout, five-card majors with a forcing 1 NT response, negative doubles. Opening two-bids are on *Acol* lines, except that it is usual now to play the *Multicoloured 2 ◇*.

FORCING BID

The following bids are played as forcing for at least one round in all popular systems:
1. A new suit in response to an opening bid (assuming that responder has not passed originally).
2. A *Reverse* by opener after a response at the two level. Any reverse by responder.
3. A new suit at the level of three.
4. A bid of the *Fourth Suit*.
5. A new suit following a raise. See *Trial Bid*.
6. A new suit after a response at the two level (1 ♡–2 ♣–2 ◇). In many systems the response at the two level of itself promises a further bid by the responder.
7. Return to partner's suit at the three level is forcing in *Acol* when both major suits have been bid (1 ♡–1 ♠–2 ♠–3 ♡), and for some

partnerships when there has been a response at the two-level (1 ♡–2 ◇–3 ◇–3 ♡). In America all such sequences are forcing.

Practice differs widely in respect of jump rebids. Generally speaking, jump rebids by responder are played as forcing, but jump rebids by opener over a response at the one-level are not.

For game-forcing bids, see *Jump Shift*.

FORCING 1 NT RESPONSE

In systems which employ five-card major openings, such as *Precision* and the more modern American systems, it is usual to play a response of 1 NT as forcing. The bid is used mostly on hands in the 6- to 12-point range where responder wishes to keep the bidding under control.

In general, the opener continues along natural lines. If however he would have passed a non-forcing response of 1 NT, he rebids in a three-card minor. This is not forcing. A rebid of opener's suit tends to suggest a six-card suit.

FORCING PASS

In a competitive auction a player may make a forcing pass whenever it is clear from the previous bidding that his partner will have to take some action. For example:

South	West	North	East
2 NT	Pass	3 ♠	4 ◇
?			

South holds:

    ♠ K 10   ♡ A K J 5   ◇ A 10 2   ♣ K Q 7 4

It is not conceivable that South should wish to defend a contract of 4 ◇ undoubled, so the best move is a forcing pass, saying, in effect, 'My hand is suitable both for defence and attack. You choose!'

At slam level a forcing pass has a special sense, connected with controls. Suppose the bidding goes:

South	West	North	East
1 ♡	1 ♠	3 ◇	4 ♠
Pass	5 ♠	6 ♡	Pass
7 ♡	Pass	Pass	7 ♠
Pass			

As the pass implies willingness to consider a higher contract, North may infer that South holds *ace* of spades, not a void, and is prepared for 7 NT.

FORCING TWO-BIDS

In standard American the opening two-bid in any suit was defined as forcing until Goren conceded the optional use of the artificial 2 ♣ opening.

In terms of the Goren point-count, the requirements for an opening two-bid are 25 points with a good five-card suit, 23 points with a good six-card suit, 21 points with a good seven-card suit. The requirements are slightly higher when the main suit is a minor. The negative response is 2 NT. For a positive response partner needs 7 points and a quick trick (ace or K–Q), or 8 points with at least a king. A double raise, 2 ♡–4 ♡, shows trump support, no ace or king, no singleton. After a negative 2 NT the responder may pass on the next round if opener can do no more than rebid his suit.

The forcing-two method has profound disadvantages: too much strain is placed on opening bids of one, it is uneconomical to use four different bids to express initially a very strong hand, and the weakness response of 2 NT is clumsy. The majority of tournament players use the more flexible 1 ♣ or 2 ♣ systems.

FORCING-TWO SYSTEM

See *Culbertson System, Forcing Two-Bids, Goren System.*

FOUR-CLUB BLACKWOOD

Some players use 4 ♣ instead of 4 NT as an enquiry for aces. Responses are on the step principle—4 ◇ shows none or four aces,

4 ♡ shows one ace, and so on. On the next round 5 ♣ asks for kings and it is possible even to ask for queens with 6 ♣.

After a 4 ♡ or 4 ♠ response to 4 ♣, 4 NT by the interrogator can be used to ask responder to identify his aces. A single ace is named, and two aces can be identified by bidding 5 ♣ for two aces of the same colour, 5 ◇ for two of the same rank (two major or two minor), 5 ♡ for 'odd' aces. The mnemonic CRO covers these responses. When clubs may be a natural suit, the partnership can revert to 4 NT as ace-enquiry.

The 4 ♣ style certainly provides a gain in space; its main disadvantage is that 4 ♣ is not available as a cue bid.

Compare *Gerber Convention*.

FOUR-NOTRUMP OPENING

The most common use of the 4 NT opening is conventional, as an immediate request for aces. The responses are:

5 ♣   no ace
5 ◇   ace of diamonds
5 ♡   ace of hearts
5 ♠   ace of spades
5 NT two aces
6 ♣   ace of clubs

The convention is sometimes known as the Acol 4 NT opening.

The responses may also follow the pattern of *Roman Blackwood*, responder bidding 5 ♡ with two aces of the same rank or colour, 5 ♠ with two aces of different rank or colour. This scheme has advantages when the 4 NT bidder holds a void.

FOURTH-HAND OPENING

At rubber bridge it is seldom advisable to open fourth in hand on less strength than is required for an opening bid in first or second hand. Strength in the major suits is an important consideration. However, the fact that the last player, like third hand, does not have to rebid over a simple response by his partner enables him to open a certain kind of borderline hand that would be passed in a different position.

♠ A Q J 4   ♡ 10 5   ◇ K J 8 4   ♣ J 7 3

This is an unattractive opening first or second hand, but in fourth position either 1 ♠ or 1 ◇ can be bid in an attempt to snatch a part score. Some players might prefer a weak notrump.

Opening bids of three and four in last position are stronger than in any other position. A player with a weak hand has no need to pre-empt: he can simply throw in. This is a typical three-bid in fourth position:

♠5 ♡K J 10 9 6 5 4 ◇A J 7 ♣J 3

Fourth hand can expect to make about nine tricks in hearts if partner has his fair share of the outstanding strength. He does not want to give the opponents a chance to come in with 1 ♠ over an opening of 1 ♡, so he opens 3 ♡.

FOURTH SUIT FORCING

When three suits have been bid by a partnership, the fourth suit seldom provides a likely spot for the final contract. Thus for many tournament players a bid of the fourth suit conveys no promise of strength in the suit named: it is simply a manoeuvre to ensure that the bidding will continue and to extract further information from partner.

South	North
1 ◇	1 ♡
2 ♣	?

North holds:

♠862 ♡A Q 8 5 3 ◇A 9 ♣K 6 3

Having no good natural call, East bids the fourth suit, 2 ♠. Partner will not call notrumps unless he himself has a guard in spades.

The level to which a bid of the fourth suit should be forcing is a debatable matter. The following scheme is suggested:

1. When a player bids the fourth suit at the level of one or two, he may pass a response that depresses him, with the proviso that support for one of his own suits should not be considered 'depressing'.

2. A bid of the fourth suit at the three level is forcing to game, at any rate so far as the responder is concerned; the fourth suit bidder

himself may stay short of game when he knows that his partner's hand is limited.

A raise of the fourth suit is in order when it can be offered below the range of 3 NT. The raise denotes four cards and hence a three-suited hand.

FRAGMENT BID

A bid of one more than a force is used, on the second round of bidding, to show support for partner's suit and a shortage in the fourth suit.

South	North
1 ♣	1 ♡
1 ♠	4 ♢

North's 4 ♢ shows a 'fragment', usually two or three cards, and it guarantees a singleton or void, in this case in clubs.

Compare *Splinter Bid*.

FREE BID, RAISE OR REBID

A free bid, raise or rebid, is one made after an overcall by the player on the right. These are examples:

	South	West	North	East
(1)	1 ♣	1 ♡	1 ♠	
(2)	1 ♡	Pass	1 ♠	2 ♣
	2 ♡			
(3)	1 ♡	1 ♠	2 ♡	

It is generally agreed that the free bid in (1) and the free rebid in (2) should not be made on minimum hands. The free raise in (3), in the traditional American practice, should denote sound values also. *Acol* players and tournament players in general tend to place less emphasis on this principle, deeming it advisable, in competition, to support on quite weak hands rather than be left out of the auction.

Special situations occur when there has been an intervening double:

South	West	North	East
1 ♡	Double	2 ♣	

The change of suit in this sequence is normally played as limited and non-forcing, but see *Take-Out Double*.

South	West	North	East
1 ♠	Double	Redouble	2 ♣
2 ♠			

Here South's rebid of 2 ♠, which denies the redoubler a chance to double 2 ♣, indicates a rather weak, distributional hand with long spades.

FREE DOUBLE

The term is used mainly of doubles of a part-score contract in rubber bridge that, if unsuccessful, would not double the opponents into game. For example, a double of 3 ♡ when opponents already have 30 on score is a 'free double'. Such gifts are not really free, however. If you double 3 ♡ and defeat non-vulnerable opponents by one trick you gain an extra 50, but if they make an overtrick you lose an extra 240.

GAMBLING 3 NT

See *Three Notrump Opening.*

GAME-FORCING OVERCALL

See *Cue-Bid Overcall.*

GARDENER NOTRUMP OVERCALL

The idea is similar to that of the Comic Notrump, which derives its name from a French phrase, *sans-atout comique*. In the Gardener version an overcall of 1 NT may be *either* a 'nonsense', such as a seven-card suit with very little high-card strength, *or* a genuine overcall in the 15–18 point range, the exact level depending on vulnerability.

The responder to a Gardener 1 NT (assuming the next player passes) may:
1. Pass if he would pass a genuine overcall.
2. If weak, with a long suit, bid this suit (on the presumption that partner has a genuine overcall). Such action is dangerous if the suit to be named is of higher range than partner's likely escape suit.

3. Bid 2 ♣, to discover the nature of the overcall. The overcaller will then bid his escape suit if he has the 'comic' type; bid the opponent's suit at the two level if he is genuine but not upper range; bid 2 NT if genuine and upper range.

GERBER CONVENTION

This convention uses a bid of 4 ♣ to ask for aces. It is possible to use the convention for this purpose in all auctions where a trump suit has been agreed or where notrumps have been bid. Many players who ordinarily use *Blackwood* play Gerber after an opening 1 NT or 2 NT, so that 4 NT will remain available as a natural raise.

4 ♣, as an immediate response to an opening 1 NT or 2 NT, asks the opener to show his aces in accordance with the step system. 4 ◇ shows no ace or four, 4 ♡ one ace, and so on.

5 ♣, following 4 ♣, asks for kings. Any other bid after the response to 4 ♣ means 'This is where we should play.'

South	North
1 NT	4 ♣ (Gerber)
4 ♠	4 NT

South's 4 ♠ call shows two aces. North's 4 NT means that he wishes to play there.

Gerber may also be used when a conventional 2 ♣ opening has been followed by a natural rebid of 2 NT, as in this sequence:

South	North
2 ♣	2 ♡
2 NT	4 ♣ (Gerber)

See, also, *Four-Club Blackwood*.

GLADIATOR CONVENTION

Developed in New Zealand, this convention is designed for responding to a 1 NT opening. It covers hands of all degrees of strength. In response to 1 NT:

2 ♣ is the prelude to a sign-off. Opener is required to bid 2 ◇ and responder now signs off in a suit (or passes).

2 ◇ is game-forcing *Stayman*. Opener shows a major suit, or bids 2 NT, or bids 3 ♣ with both majors.

2 ♡ and 2 ♠ are game-forcing and show five-card suits.

Three-level responses invite a slam.

Four-level responses also show slam hopes, but with a six-card or longer suit headed by the jack at best.

GOREN SYSTEM

The methods of bidding recommended by Charles Goren have become standard in North America and correspond closely to the standard methods described in this book. Where there is a difference between American and British practice, both are described.

For the Goren method of valuation, see *Distributional Point Count*.

GRAND SLAM FORCE

This is a conventional method of locating the top cards in the trump suit when a grand slam at a suit contract is under investigation. It is often called 'Josephine' after Culbertson's wife, who first described it in a *Bridge World* article.

A direct bid of 5 NT, not preceded by 4 NT, is a grand slam force, asking partner about his holding in the trump suit. Partner is invited to bid seven in the agreed suit if he holds two of the top three trump honours (ace, king, queen).

This system of responses to 5 NT is open to considerable improvement. In *Bridge for Tournament Players* the present authors recommend the following system. The responder to 5 NT bids:

6 ♣ no top honour (A, K or Q)
6 ◇ one top honour
6 ♡ two top honours
6 ♠ three top honours

The convention will now serve a player who needs to find partner with, say, the king of trumps; or a player who wants to be in seven only if partner has A K Q.

For a different form of trump asking bid, see *Baron Grand Slam Try*.

HERBERT CONVENTION

This term describes the convention originally devised by Walter Herbert for the Vienna system. A bid of the next higher-ranking suit is the negative response to certain forcing bids or to a take-out double. As mentioned under *Acol System*, Herbert responses can be used in place of the traditional 2 NT when responding to a two-bid.

South	North
2 ◇	<u>2 ♡</u>

Here 2 ♡ is a negative response. A notable advantage is that the strong hand can rebid at notrumps.

HONOUR TRICKS

An honour trick is a card or a combination of cards that may reasonably be expected to win an early trick, even against an opponent's trump contract. Thus an ace or K Q is reckoned as one honour trick, A K as two, A Q as $1\frac{1}{2}$, K x as $\frac{1}{2}$. The Culbertson system used honour tricks as a method of hand valuation. An opening bid of one promised $2\frac{1}{2}$ honour tricks, slightly above a player's normal expectation, and a minimum of 5 tricks was required for a forcing-two opening. This method of valuation has been almost universally superseded by point-count.

INFORMATORY DOUBLE

This is the old term for *Take-out Double*.

INVERTED MINOR SUIT RAISES

The term describes the practice of making the raise of 1 ♣ to 2 ♣, or 1 ◇ to 2 ◇, constructive, and a double raise, 1 ♣–3 ♣, or 1 ◇–3 ◇, pre-emptive. In the *Kaplan-Sheinwold System* the single raise is forcing, with a range of 9–20 points.

JUMP OVERCALL

A jump overcall is a suit overcall one trick higher than the minimum level. For example:

South	West	North	East
Pass	Pass	1 ◇	2 ♠

For most British players the jump overcall shows the equivalent of a sound opening and a good six-card suit but is not forcing. The standard American practice is to use the jump overcall as a mild pre-empt on a weak hand with a long suit. (See *Weak Jump Overcall*.) There are also some special conventional overcalls, such as *Roman Jump Overcalls*.

JUMP PREFERENCE

A return to partner's first suit at one range higher than necessary is described as jump preference. These are typical sequences:

	South	North
(1)	1 ♡	1 ♠
	2 ♣	3 ♡
(2)	1 ♠	2 ♢
	2 ♡	3 ♠
(3)	1 ♢	1 ♡
	1 ♠	3 ♢

These sequences are not forcing in *Acol*, but would be regarded as forcing by most American players.

JUMP RAISE

See *Double Raise of Suit Opening*.

JUMP REBID

The term is normally used of a jump in the player's own first suit, as in these sequences:

South	North
1 ♢	1 ♡
3 ♢	

This rebid, after partner's one-level response, is non-forcing.

1 ♠	2 ♣
3 ♠	

As partner has responded at the two level, this rebid is forcing for most players. In any system the opener would *expect* the bidding to continue, but if responder had a long suit of clubs which he was intending to rebid at the three level he might deem it advisable to pass.

$$1 \heartsuit \qquad 1 \spadesuit$$
$$2 \diamondsuit \qquad \underline{3 \spadesuit}$$

The standard practice is to treat this jump rebid *by the responder* as forcing both in Britain and America.

JUMP SHIFT

A jump bid in a new suit is unconditionally forcing to game in all standard systems. In response to an opening bid, the requirements for a jump shift vary according to system. In *Acol* it is normal to force with 16 points in high cards, or with less when game appears to be certain; in America the jump shift is almost a slam invitation, indicating at least 19 points including distribution.

Many tournament players follow a style whereby an immediate force indicates either excellent support for opener or a more or less self-supporting suit. With a two-suiter, responder does not force on the first round. It follows that a sequence such as 1 ◇–2 ♡–2 NT–3 ♣ is likely to be based either on strong hearts and a club control or on strong diamonds and a club control.

A special meaning may be attached to a jump shift when a bid at a lower level would have been forcing:

South	North
1 ♡	2 ♣
3 ♠	

Here 2 ♠, a reverse after a response at the two level, would have been forcing. The jump to 3 ♠ now suggests support for clubs and control in spades. See *Fragment Bid* and *Splinter Bid*.

KAPLAN-SHEINWOLD SYSTEM

The main features of this system, devised by Edgar Kaplan and Alfred Sheinwold, are: weak notrump throughout, five-card majors with a forcing 1 NT response, weak two-bids, responses at the two level forcing to 2 NT. In different versions of the system, opening major suit bids have been played as 'possibly light, about 9 points with a fair suit', and as controlled psychics, 3 to 6 points, preferably on a 5-card suit containing a high honour.

KOCK-WERNER REDOUBLE

See *SOS Redouble.*

LANDY CONVENTION

This is one of the many methods devised for competing against an opponent's 1 NT opening. An overcall of 2 ♣ promises a minimum of nine cards in the major suits and general strength insufficient for a double. The normal range, depending on vulnerability and the strength of the opposing notrump, is from about 9 points (with 5–5 in the majors) to 15. Some players use the convention only in second hand against a weak notrump, but it can be used in fourth hand also, and against a strong notrump. The only forcing response to a Landy overcall of 2 ♣ is 3 ♣.

See, also, the defensive systems listed under *Astro.*

LEAD-DIRECTING DOUBLES

By convention the double of a slam contract, other than an obvious sacrifice, is lead-directing. (See *Lightner Double.*) At the game level the double of 3 NT by the player sitting over the dummy is also lead-directing, or at any rate lead-suggesting, with the priorities as follows:

1. When the doubler has bid a suit, he asks for that suit.
2. When the opening leader (but not the doubler) has bid a suit, the double exhorts him to lead that suit.
3. When the defenders have not bid, the double asks for a lead of the first suit bid by dummy. (But the leader must use his judgement: if the suit has been rebid, especially, the doubler is likely to hold tricks in the suit but will not want it to be led.)
4. When no suit has been bid, as in 1 NT–3 NT, the double beseeches the leader to find the doubler's long suit. Thus East, holding ♠ K Q J 10 x and a side ace, might double South's 3 NT, and West, with a singleton spade perhaps, should lead this suit.

LEAD-INHIBITING BIDS

These are tactical bids, in the nature of mild psychic bids, designed to prevent a damaging lead. For example:

♠ K J x   ♡ K J x   ◇ A x x   ♣ Q 10 x x

The straightforward approach with this hand is to open 1 ♣ and to rebid 1 NT over a simple suit response. An opening of 1 ◇, made with the idea of discouraging a diamond lead against a notrump contract, would be a lead-inhibiting bid.

Lead-inhibiting bids are sometimes made on the way to a slam contract:

♠ K x x x x   ♡ —   ◇ A K x x x x   ♣ x x

Over partner's opening of 1 ♠, responder may elect to bid 2 ♣ or 3 ♣.

LEBENSOHL CONVENTION

This is a scheme for third hand after opener's 1 NT has been overcalled by second hand. There are three main situations:

1. *Natural overcall*, e.g. North 1 NT, East 2 ♡. Now 2 ♠ by South is competitive, any suit at the three level is forcing. The distinctive feature of the convention is that 2 NT commands opener to rebid 3 ♣. Responder may then pass or bid 3 ◇ (competitive) or 3 ♠ (invitational). The scheme also permits responder to distinguish between a raise to 3 NT that contains a guard in the enemy suit and a raise that does not. The direct raise disclaims a guard; 2 NT, followed by 3 NT on the next round, promises a guard. A double shows the values for a natural raise to 2 NT; but of course it is possible to double on a stronger hand, as the doubler can control matters.

2. *Conventional overcall, identifying one suit only*, as in Astro, where an overcall of 2 ◇ would indicate spades and a minor suit. Now a double of 2 ◇ implies the values to double 2 ♠; 2 ♠ shows values in the other three suits; and 2 NT and double are used in the same sense as above.

3. *Conventional overcall, identifying two suits*, as in Landy, where 2 ♣ denotes the majors. Now a double is penalty-oriented against at least one of the suits shown by the overcall, a cue bid of the lower suit (hearts) is less strong than a cue bid of the higher suit (spades), and 2 NT and double have the same sense as above.

LIGHTNER DOUBLE

In this universal convention a double of a freely-bid slam asks for an *unexpected* lead, which may be a suit bid by the dummy, or a suit bid by the declarer, or a suit in which a void is held. In any case, the leader is dissuaded from making a neutral or obvious lead, such as a trump, or a suit bid by the defending side, or the only unbid suit. By extension, an 'unlikely' double of a game contract may contain the same message.

LITTLE MAJOR

This system, devised principally by Terence Reese, was an early essay in the relay principle. The general sense of opening bids was as follows:

- 1 ♣: club suit; a response of 1 ◇ either negative or the first move on a strong hand. (This duality could be, but so far has not been, attached to any 1 ♣ system.)
- 1 ◇: either a spade suit or a strong notrump, 17–19 points; a response of 1 ♡ either negative or the first move on a strong hand.
- 1 ♡: either a strong hand, 20 upwards, or a balanced 3 to 6.
- 1 ♠: main values in the minor suits.
- 1 NT: natural, 14 to 16.
- 2 ♣: natural, no four-card major.
- 2 ◇: natural, no four-card major.
- 2 ♡, 2 ♠: varieties of major-minor two-suiter.
- 2 NT: pre-emptive type with a long minor.

The system attracted considerable attention in the early 1960s, but as developed by Terence Reese and Jeremy Flint it became increasingly complicated and (owing to licensing restrictions) opportunities to play it were infrequent.

LOSING TRICK COUNT

Primarily a method of valuation, the Losing Trick Count was made the basis for a bidding system by an American writer, Dudley Courtenay. When a satisfactory trump fit—usually a 4–4 or 5–3 combination—has been found, each player counts his losers as follows:

1. Count one loser for each missing high honour (A, K or Q) in each suit, up to a maximum of three in any suit. Thus A x x x x counts as two losers; the K Q are missing, but the fourth and fifth cards are not counted as losers.
2. Losers in short suits are counted only up to the number of worthless cards held. Thus a singleton other than the ace is one loser; a small doubleton is two losers; A x and K x are also one loser, but Q x is two losers. A void or singleton ace counts as no losers.

Rule of Eighteen

A sound minimum opening is assumed to contain seven losers. A responder who raises his partner's opening may add the losers in his own hand to the opener's expected seven losers. The total is deducted from 18 and the resulting figure gives the number of odd tricks that may be expected. For example:

Opener	*Responder*
♠K 10 9 6 3	♠Q 8 4 2
♡K Q 7 2	♡9 5
◇K 9 7	◇A 10 3
♣4	♣K J 8 3

The opening bid is 1 ♠ and the responder, with good support for this suit, assesses his losers, eight in all. Adding this figure to the seven expected in opener's hand, and deducting the total from 18, he raises to 3 ♠.

Opener, too, may apply the Losing Trick Count when rebidding. Here he has only six losers—two in spades, one in hearts, two in diamonds and one in clubs. As partner has shown eight losers, he deducts the total from 18 and raises to 4 ♠, just worth bidding on the two hands.

LOWER MINOR CONVENTION

This is one of the many methods proposed as a defence against pre-emptive bids. Over a weak three opening a bid of the cheaper minor by the next player is a request for a take-out.

South	*West*	*North*	*East*
—	—	3 ♣	3 ◇

South	*West*	*North*	*East*
—	—	3 ♡	4 ♣

In each case East is asking West to show a suit.

The convention is not used by a player sitting under the three bidder, as in this position it is standard to use double for take-out.

An advantage of the Lower Minor convention is that both double and 3 NT have their natural sense. On the other hand, to bid 4 ♣ for take-out over 3 ◇ or 3 ♡ causes serious loss of space, and for this reason many players use the convention over 3 ♣ only.

MATHEMATICS OF RUBBER BRIDGE

In rubber bridge there are hidden values that do not appear on the score-sheet. Thus a side scores nothing above the line for its first game, but this game obviously has a mathematical value. Similarly, a part score is worth more than the points actually shown on the score-sheet. In order to judge the extent of the risks that he may take in competitive bidding, a player needs to be able to assess these unseen values.

Hidden value of game

1. *When neither side is vulnerable*, the hidden value of the first game is theoretically 350 points. This is because the side scoring the first game has a 50 per cent chance of winning a 700-point rubber, while the remaining possibilities cancel out. (That is to say, this side has a 25 per cent chance of winning a 500 rubber and a 25 per cent chance of losing one.)

To this hidden value of 350 points must be added the visible value of the trick score, let us say 120, giving a total of 470. On the other hand, the side that is not vulnerable has an advantage because it can bid with greater freedom. This factor cannot be exactly assessed, but it is generally reckoned that the true value of the first game is about 420 points, as against the theoretical figure of 470.

It follows that it shows only a slight loss to concede a penalty of 500 to save the first game of a rubber, and a slight gain to save at the expense of only 300.

2. *When one side is a game up*, the value of the equalizing game is the same as the value of the first game, 420, since it eliminates the advantage that the vulnerable pair has acquired. Thus, it does not pay the side that is a game up to go down 500 to prevent the opponents from drawing even.

To the vulnerable pair, the value of the rubber game is just short of 500 points. The rubber may amount to 900 points or so, but 420 of those points were already 'in the bank', as was shown under (1). It follows that, not vulnerable against vulnerable, a side that goes down 500 to save a game shows a slight loss.

3. *When both sides are vulnerable* the value of the game is accurately represented on the score-sheet. To go down 500 to save the game now shows a profit, for the opponents would have recorded 500 plus the trick score.

Hidden value of part score

In duplicate bridge 50 points are added for all part-score contracts, but there is no doubt that at rubber bridge the hidden value of a part score of 40 or more is greater than that. The figure cannot be calculated mathematically, for there are too many imponderable factors. It is probably right to say that the hidden value ranges from about 70 with no one vulnerable to as much as 200 at game all.

The trick score, averaging about 60, must be added to the hidden value when a part-score battle is in progress. To prevent opponents from making a part score is therefore worth about 130 to 260, according to the vulnerability.

The hidden value of a part score has a bearing also on sacrifice bidding at the game level. A side that has 60 below can afford to defend the game with additional spirit, whereas the side whose opponents have the part score should be less willing to incur a penalty. For some reason, the majority of players construe the matter in an opposite sense.

Mathematics of slam bidding

A small slam, not vulnerable, is rewarded by an extra 500. If it fails by one trick the loss is also about 500 (300 game equity plus about 150 trick score, plus 50 penalty), so the small slam is an even proposition.

Vulnerable against not vulnerable, the small slam brings in 750. The loss is about 650 (400 game equity plus 150 for tricks, plus 100 penalty), so the slam is worth bidding at slight odds against.

With both sides vulnerable the slam still brings in 750 but the loss is nearly 750, so it is again about an even proposition. (In these calculations it is assumed that the slam bid is in a major suit or in notrumps.)

In short, the most favourable moment for a small slam is when vulnerable against not vulnerable.

The extra bonus for a grand slam, not vulnerable, is 500; the loss, as against a small slam made, about 1,000; so odds of two to one in favour are required. The figure is much the same in other vulnerability positions.

A common fallacy

It is worth remarking that players who, having sustained a heavy penalty and won the rubber later, say 'It didn't cost us anything' are deluding themselves. The merit or otherwise of a sacrifice bid or a slam call is determined on that deal alone and is unaffected by subsequent happenings.

For the mathematics of doubling and redoubling, see *Penalty Double* and *Redouble*.

MICHAELS CUE BID

This convention gives better employment to immediate overcalls in an opponent's suit than are present in the 'giant' cue bids of traditional systems. A cue bid in an opponent's minor suit indicates a limited hand with at least nine cards in the major suits.

♠KJ853　♡KJ92　◇72　♣106

Overcall 1♣ with 2♣ or 1◇ with 2◇.

Over a major-suit opening the Michaels cue bid shows the unbid major suit and an unspecified minor suit. There is now no upper limit of strength: the cue bidder may have a powerful hand on which he plans to take further action.

The responder bids the full value of his hand when there is a known fit. New-suit responses to the cue bid are not forcing. With a strong hand but no immediate fit, responder may seek clarification by a repeat cue bid in the enemy suit.

Other conventional overcalls showing two-suited hands are *Astro Cue Bid* and *Roman Jump Overcalls*.

MILTON WORK COUNT

The popular point-count of numbers—4 for an ace, 3 for a king, 2 for a queen, and 1 for a jack—is associated with the name of the American writer, Milton C. Work.

Aces are somewhat undervalued in this count, and queens overvalued. However, the simplicity of the count ensures its continued popularity.

MINI-NOTRUMP

At tournament bridge the use of a 10 to 12 point notrump opening in first or second position, not vulnerable, has been found a playable method. The established scheme of responses remains, *mutatis mutandis.*

MOYSIAN FIT

To play in 4 ♡ or 4 ♠ with a 4–3 fit in the trump suit is to play in the Moysian Fit. The American editor, Alphonse Moyse Jr., considered that bidding technique was insufficiently directed towards such contracts.

MULTICOLOURED 2 ◇

This convention, first expounded in depth by Terence Reese, has been very widely adopted by tournament players because it combines two important objectives: economy in the use of bids and confusion of the opponents. An opening 2 ◇ (in the original version) stands for one of the following: (*a*) A weak two-bid in spades or hearts, normally 7 to 11 points with a five-card suit; or (*b*) an opening 2 NT, slightly stronger than a direct 2 NT; or (*c*) a strong three-suiter, containing both major suits. (This style works best when a 1 ♣ system is played.)

Responses

Responder assumes initially that the bid reflects a weak two in the majors. His responses have the following meaning:

2 ♡   'If you have a weak two in hearts, this is where we play.'
2 ♠   'If you have a weak two in spades, this is where we play.'
2 NT 'Forcing, tell me your type and range.'
3 ♣, 3 ◇ 'Strong suit, may be the best contract.'
3 ♡, 3 ♠ 'Strong suit, invitation to game.'
3 NT 'Strong minor two-suiter.'

Rebids

Opener's rebids depend on which type he holds. These are the principal sequences:

1. *Opener has weak two in one of the majors.* Over 2 ♠, if opener holds hearts, he bids 3 ♣ (permitting partner to pass this or to bid 3 ◇, non-forcing). Over 2 NT he bids 3 ♣ to show hearts, upper range, 3 ◇ to show spades, upper range, 3 ♡ or 3 ♠ with lower range.

2. *Opener has 2 NT type.* In all cases he rebids at minimum level in notrumps.

3. *Opener has 3-suiter type with both majors.* He rebids 3 ♡ when his minor suit is clubs, 3 ♠ when it is diamonds.

Defence to the Multi

When opponents are playing the Multi, the following scheme of defence is playable:

1. *Action by second hand over the 2 ◇ opening.* Double signifies a take-out double of spades, 2 ♡ a take-out double of hearts, 2 ♠ is natural, and 2 NT suggests the equivalent of an opening strong notrump.

2. *Action by fourth hand when responder has bid 2 ♡.* Double is a take-out double of hearts, 2 ♠ and 2 NT are natural. (With a take-out double of spades fourth hand can wait for the next round.)

3. *Action by fourth hand when responder has bid 2 ♠.* Double is a take-out double of spades, 2 NT is natural.

NEAPOLITAN SYSTEM

This system was the forerunner of, and very similar to, the *Blue Club System*.

NEGATIVE DOUBLE

This style of double, known also as 'Sputnik' because it was introduced at the time of the first Russian satellite, is very common in tournament play. A double of intervention over an opening suit bid is not for penalties but has the character of a take-out double. The bidding goes:

South	West	North	East
1 ◇	1 ♠	Dble	

North's double proclaims initially about 7 to 10 points, with no obvious call. He should have fair support for hearts, the 'other major'. In the same way, the double of an overcall in hearts promises support for spades. The opener rebids on this assumption.

It is usual to play negative doubles up to the level of 3 ♡. Thus 1 ♠–3 ♡ (weak jump overcall)–double signifies all-round values but not good support for spades.

When the responder is strong in the suit of the overcall his best action usually is to pass. Some partnerships treat the pass as virtually forcing on the opener.

The effect on suit responses

The usefulness of negative doubles can be increased by making certain adjustments in the forcing quality of suit bids by the responder. Compare these sequences:

	South	West	North	East
(1)	1 ♡	2 ♣	2 ◇	
(2)	1 ♡	2 ♣	2 ♠	
(3)	1 ♠	2 ♡	3 ◇	

In (1) North has bid a lower-valued suit than opener's and the response has its normal forcing quality. In (2) North is bidding a suit of higher value. The understanding here should be that 2 ♠ is non-forcing; with spades and a good hand North would double first and bid again on the next round. Similarly, in (3), North's bid at the three level is best played as non-forcing; with a better hand North would double 2 ♡ and correct later.

When a player doubles and follows with a free bid on the next round, the initial message is cancelled. For example:

South	West	North	East
1 ♣	1 ♡	Dble	Pass
2 ♠	Pass	3 ◇	

North's double of 1 ♡ implies initially a limited hand with four spades. South, holding four spades, rebids on the assumption that his partner has this type. When North follows with 3 ◇ he shows a different type altogether—a good hand with a diamond suit.

It is possible, also, to play negative doubles when 1 NT has been overcalled. South opens 1 NT and West overcalls with 2 ♡; now a double by North shows values but no stop in hearts.

NOTTINGHAM SYSTEM

Of the many 1 ♣ systems that were popular in the early days of contract, this is one of the few that have survived. It is played mainly in the Midlands and North of England.

Except for hands that are opened with 2 ◊ or 2 NT, all hands containing 16 or more points are opened with 1 ♣. The negative response with less than eight points is 1 ◊.

A 2 ◊ opening shows a minimum of 22 points. Openings of 1 ♡, 1 ♠ and 2 ♣ are natural, showing at least a five-card suit and 12 to 15 points. 1 NT is bid on a balanced 13 to 15 points. An opening 1 ◊ serves for all other limited hands not containing a five-card major.

Modern players may note that the *Precision System* has a very similar structure.

NOTRUMP OVERCALL

An overcall of 1 NT by second hand shows a strong balanced hand with at least one guard in the opponent's suit and 15 to 18 points. For 1 NT in fourth position, see *Balancing*. In *Baron* the overcall is played as a weak take-out double.

A direct overcall of 2 NT, for most players, is the *Unusual Notrump*. With a powerful balanced hand, too strong for a 1 NT overcall, the practice is to double first and bid notrumps on the next round. In fourth position an overcall of 2 NT is natural, but probably based on a strong minor suit.

NOTRUMP RESPONSES TO SUIT OPENING

1 NT response

The response of 1 NT to an opening 1 ◊, 1 ♡ or 1 ♠ suggests about 6 to 9 points. The range over 1 ♣ is slightly higher, more like 7 to 10.

2 NT response

This can be played as a limit bid, *Acol* style, about 11 to 12, or as forcing, American style, about 13 to 15.

3 NT response

The range in American systems is usually 16 to 18, in British systems 13 to 15. As 3 NT tends to be an awkward response for an opener with a five-card major and a singleton, some partnerships lay down that the bid should be made only with 4–3–3–3 distribution, so that the opener can always be assured of three-card support in his long suit.

OGUST REBIDS

These rebids are for use by a player who has opened with a weak two in a major suit. Over the forcing response of 2 NT, opener rebids as follows:

3 ♣ lower range, moderate suit.
3 ◇ upper range, moderate suit.
3 ♡ lower range, good suit.
3 ♠ upper range, good suit.

In the *Blue Club* the sense of 3 ◇ and 3 ♡ is reversed and the mnemonic, P before Q, signifying Points before Quality (of suit), is then applicable. The mnemonic for Ogust rebids might be R before S, Range before Suit.

ONE-CLUB SYSTEMS

Systems employing a strong 1 ♣ opening include *Blue Club, Nottingham System, Precision System*. In the *Vienna System* 1 ♣ is a comparatively weak opening and in the *Roman System* it may be weak or strong.

ONE-NOTRUMP OPENING

Most players follow one of three styles: *Weak notrump throughout* (12 to 14); *strong notrump throughout* (may be 15 to 17, 16 to 18, 17 to 19); *variable*, usually 12 to 14 not vulnerable, 15 to 17 vulnerable. The stronger ranges are more common in America, the weaker ranges in Britain.

The following entries are concerned with responses to opening bids in notrumps: *Gerber, Gladiator, Stayman, Transfer Bids*.

OPENING SUIT BIDS OF ONE

In systems that do not use a strong 1 ♣ opening, the normal range for an opening suit bid of one is from 12 to 20 points. With a strong six-card suit, or a well constructed 5–5 type, the point-count may be no higher than 10 or 11.

Choice of suits

With two biddable suits the general rules are:

1. Between five-card suits of equal length, begin with the higher-ranking, except that with clubs and spades 1 ♣ is usually preferred.
2. Between five- and six-card suits, generally bid the longer, except that when the suits are adjacent the higher may be preferred.
3. Between four- and five-card suits, bid the higher first, except on limited hands of this type:

♠A x   ♡x x   ◇A K J 9   ♣Q 10 x x x

Here 1 ◇ is sounder than 1 ♣. See *Reverse Bid*.

4. When only four-card suits are held, the general policy is to bid the suit 'below' the doubleton. Thus with 4–3–4–2 you open 1 ♠, so that you can deal with any response; with 4–2–4–3 open 1 ◇ so that over 1 ♡ you can bid 1 ♠. (Different considerations arise, of course, when *Five-Card Majors* are played.)
5. On 4–4–4–1 types there is a general rule in favour of bidding the suit below the singleton; but the quality of the suits always has a bearing.

OPTIONAL DOUBLE

The term is most often used in connection with the double by second hand of an opponent's pre-emptive opening. It means, literally, that partner has the option to pass or take out, but by some semantic accident a so-called optional double tends to be primarily for take-out.

OVERCALL

A simple overcall is a bid at the minimum level, such as 1 ♠ over 1 ◇ or 2 ♣ over 1 ♠, after an opponent has opened the bidding. There is no fixed lower limit, and overcalls that deprive the opponent of bidding space, such as 1 ♠ over 1 ♣, are often made on no more than seven or eight points. The upper limit of strength is about equal to a sound minimum opening; with stronger hands it is usual to double first. Most overcalls are based on at least a five-card suit but an overcall of 1 ♠, especially when shutting out a response of 1 ♡, may be made on a four-card suit.

Responding to overcalls

The responder does not usually seek a game unless he himself has opening values or strong support for partner's suit. A take-out into a new suit is not forcing and suggests inability to support overcaller's suit to the three level. Raises, even double raises, of the overcaller's suit may be made on three-card or even, when the overcall is at the two level, on two-card support. A jump shift is usually played as forcing for one round.

In responding to an overcall it is possible to play a cue bid of opener's suit as two-way in this type of sequence:

South	*West*	*North*	*East*
1 ♡	1 ♠	Pass	2 ♡

East's 2 ♡ may be a traditional force to game or it may denote merely a sound raise to 2 ♠, with fair high-card strength. The overcaller proceeds initially on this last assumption. See *Unassuming Cue Bids*.

PART-SCORE BIDDING

There are some general understandings that relate to bidding in part-score situations:

1. *Opening bids on strong hands.* It is usual to lower slightly the requirements for opening bids that would normally be forcing, such as an *Acol* two-bid. If the bid is enough for game, responder may pass, especially when opener might have forced with a conventional 2 ♣.

2. *Opening 1 NT.* With a part score of 60 or more there is tactical advantage in widening the range for 1 NT. The limits for a (nominally) weak notrump become about 12 to 18 points, for a strong notrump 15 to 20.

3. *Choice of suit opening.* Generally, there is advantage in opening in a high-ranking suit, such as 1 ♠, in preference to a minor. The

higher bid has more pre-emptive value and it is unnecessary to prepare a sound rebid.

4. *Tactics on borderline hands.* It is right to take the initiative when possible in part-score situations except perhaps when the opponents have the part score and your own hand contains no length in spades—always the important suit in any competitive battle that may follow. It is certainly safer to open 1 NT as dealer on a 12-point hand than to pass and later contest against an opponent's opening.

5. *Responder's action on weak hands.* Responder may keep the bidding open on 4 points when 1 NT would be enough for game, but to bid on less contains more risk than to pass. A response of 1 NT, when not enough for game, is non-forcing and should be avoided on any medium hand of 9 points or more when there is an alternative.

6. *Responder's action on good hands.* Any jump shift, such as 2 ♠ in response to 1 ♦ at 40 up, is unconditionally forcing on opener; and the responder himself is expected to bid at least once more. A raise from, say, 1 ♡ to 3 ♡ at 60 up should be regarded as similar to a normal limit raise. It is not purely pre-emptive, but it is also not of itself a slam suggestion.

PASSED HAND

A simple change of suit by a passed hand is not normally played as forcing. A jump shift is forcing for one round and is generally based on a fit in opener's suit.

For special conventions, see *Drury Convention* and *SNAP*.

PENALTY DOUBLE

For the distinction between a penalty double and a take-out double, see *Take-out Double.* For the significance of a double after a pre-emptive opening, see *Pre-emptive Bid.*

Mathematics of the penalty double

In all close situations the odds are weighted against the doubler to a greater extent than many players realize. For example, a borderline double of a major-suit game when declarer is not vulnerable will cost 170 points if the contract is just made and will gain only 50 if it is down one. Thus, at rubber bridge, the doubler is laying 7 to 2 on his being right.

PENALTY PASS

When a player passes his partner's take-out double because he is strong in the suit doubled, he is said to make a penalty pass.

South	West	North	East
1 ♠	Dble	Pass	Pass

Sitting under the bidder, East should be long and strong in the trump suit, preferably Q J 10 8 x x or better. It is almost a convention that, if the double is passed, West should lead a trump.

PHANTOM SACRIFICE (OR PHANTOM SAVE)

A colloquial name for a sacrifice bid that proves to be an unnecessary expense because the opponents could not have made their contract.

PLAYING TRICKS

Playing tricks are tricks that a hand may reasonably be expected to take when playing at its own best trump suit. Thus, the following hand appears to contain about eight playing tricks in spades:

♠K Q J 9 x x ♡K x ◇A K x ♣K x

Given average luck, this hand would win five spade tricks, two diamond tricks and one in hearts or clubs.

The assessment of playing tricks is especially important when a player is considering an overcall or a pre-emptive bid. See *Rule of Two and Three.*

PODI

See *Blackwood Convention.*

POINT COUNT

This is the popular way to measure the strength of a hand by allocating a point-value to each honour card and to distributional features. See *Distributional Point Count* and *Milton Work Count.*

POSITIVE RESPONSE

This is the general term for a response to an opening forcing bid that shows more than the minimum on which it would be proper to give a negative response. For the requirements in different systems, see *Forcing Two-Bids, Two-Club Opening*, and the various methods noted under *One-Club Systems*.

PRECISION SYSTEM

Precision, which has been adopted by many of the world's top players, is a 1 ♣ system with a weak notrump throughout and five-card majors. These are the main opening sequences:

1 ♣   Conventional, 16 points upwards. *Responses*: 1 ◇, 0–7; 1 ♡, 1 ♠, 2 ♣ and 2 ◇ are positive, 8 upwards, with a five-card suit; 1 NT, 8–10; 2 ♡, 2 ♠, semi-positive, long suit, 3–6.

1 ◇   12–15, often a 3-card suit. Raise to 2 ◇ stronger than a raise to 3 ◇, other responses natural.

1 ♡, 1 ♠   12–15, five-card suit in principle. Response of 1 NT forcing for one round.

1 NT   13–15 throughout. Any established scheme of responses may be attached.

2 ♣   12–15, fair suit. *Responses*: 2 ◇ conventional, 2 ♡, 2 ♠ invitational, 2 NT natural.

2 ◇   3-suiter or semi-3-suiter, with various systems of responses.

2 ♡, 2 ♠   Weak two-bid, 7–10 with a good suit. Response of 2 NT conventional.

3 ♣   Strong suit, at least one stopper outside.

Pre-emptive bids above this level are similar to those in other systems.

Precision is a developing system that has attracted many keen theorists, so there are many different versions and specialized sequences. In particular, an elaborate (and ever-changing) system of asking bids has been devised for sequences following a positive response to 1 ♣. This is sometimes called Super Precision.

PRE-EMPTIVE BID

A pre-emptive bid is one that seeks to buy the contract before the opponents have been able to exchange information. Its purpose is defensive and obstructive.

Pre-emptive openings

In almost all systems an opening 3 ♥ or 3 ♠ is a weak shut-out, based on a long suit with little or no outside strength. In general, a player will overbid by two tricks when vulnerable, by three tricks when not vulnerable, but in tournament bridge these safety limits are often relaxed.

In most systems 3 ♣ and 3 ◊ openings are similarly pre-emptive, but in the 1 ♣ systems 3 ♣ may be fairly strong.

Opening bids of 4 ♥ and 4 ♠ are pre-emptive in all systems. Many players use the *Texas Convention*, in which 4 ♣ and 4 ◊ are conventional transfer bids, stronger than a direct 4 ♥ or 4 ♠; but 4 ♣ and 4 ◊ may also be played as natural pre-empts.

Pre-emptive overcalls and responses

Any double-jump overcall (3 ♥ over 1 ◊) or double-jump response (3 ♠ in response to 1 ♣) is pre-emptive in standard practice, though it is possible to attach different meanings to the double jump in a constructive auction (see *Splinter Bid*).

Defence to pre-emptive openings

Various conventions have been devised to compete against an opponent's three-bid (or weak two-bid). See *Fishbein Convention, Lower Minor Convention, Optional Double* and *Three Notrump Take-out*.

Over an opening 4 ♠, double is for penalties; the only take-out is 4 NT (or 5 ♠ on a pronounced two-suiter). A double of 4 ♥ is primarily for penalties, but many players have the understanding that the double should contain at least tolerance for spades; in other words, responder with long spades should be free to remove the double. A double of a pre-emptive 4 ♣ or 4 ◊ is co-operative: it should be based on all-round strength.

PREFERENCE BID

A player is said to give preference, as opposed to giving support, when he shows preference for one of his partner's suits at the lowest level:

South	North
1 ◇	1 ♠
2 ♡	3 ◇

Here 3 ◇, though it takes the bidding a range higher, is simple preference. North could express weak preference for hearts only by passing. 3 ♡ would be a raise.

See also *False Preference* and *Jump Preference*.

PREPARED BID

A player who opens with one of a suit is expected to have a sound rebid over any response in a new suit. When this consideration influences the choice of opening, the player is said to make a prepared bid. See *Opening Suit Bids of One* and *Short Club*.

PRINCIPLE OF FAST ARRIVAL

The term expresses the idea that when the partnership is bound to reach a certain level, a jump that excludes enquiry should indicate limited values. A homely illustration occurs in the sequence 2 NT–4 ♠, generally played as weaker than 2 NT–3 ♠.

The Principle of Fast Arrival has a wide application in the 1 ♣ systems where a forcing-to-game (or forcing to 2 NT) situation is often established early:

South	North
1 ♣	1 ♠
2 NT	

South's 2 NT, following the idea set out above, will indicate a flat minimum, consistent with the 1 ♣ opening. With a better hand he would rebid 1 NT, leaving room for conventional enquiry. In the same way a raise to 2 ♠ would be, or might be, stronger than a raise to three or four.

PROTECTIVE BID

See *Balancing*.

PSYCHIC BID

In the widest sense, any bid that deliberately misrepresents a player's holding may be called a psychic bid. The term is generally applied, however, to an opening bid or overcall that either pretends to non-existent values or names a suit that is not the true one.

The usual occasion for such a bluff is when it seems likely that opponents have the balance of strength and, left to themselves, will reach game or slam. Thus, the psychist is usually more active when partner has passed and the vulnerability is favourable. Most psychists like to have an escape suit, to which they propose to retreat if they are doubled in their psychic suit. The more intrepid, however, do not regard an escape suit as an essential qualification.

There was a considerable vogue for psychic bids in the early days of contract, but the general improvement in bidding has made such tactics less profitable. Modern psychists, in the tournament field at any rate, conduct the battle with three-card suits, lead-inhibiting bids, and other tactical strokes. They go for gentle deflection rather than flagrant deception.

PSYCHIC CONTROLS

Some American systems, such as *Kaplan-Sheinwold* and the original *Roth-Stone*, make provision for psychic openings on very weak hands, about 2 to 6 points. A psychic control is a safety device, to prevent the bidding from getting out of hand after such an opening.

In Kaplan-Sheinwold, for example, where opening psychics are lead-directing, a jump shift response asks the opener to rebid in his suit or in notrumps, whichever is cheaper, if his opening is psychic. Any other rebid shows that the opening was genuine.

Psychic controls may be disallowed by committees responsible for Rules and Ethics.

QUANTITATIVE 4 NT

Almost all players use 4 NT in a conventional sense, but there are times when they would prefer this bid to be natural or 'quantitative'. It is a question of emphasis. For some players 4 NT is a fixed light in the heavens—*Blackwood* unless it can be proved otherwise. For others the bid is conventional only if clearly it must be. The following scheme inclines towards the second style. 4 NT is natural in the following circumstances:

1. When no genuine suit has been mentioned by either partner. This understanding is more or less universal. For the occasions when, over a notrump opening, responder wants only to know about aces, see *Gerber Convention*.

2. When no trump suit has been agreed, directly or by inference, and 4 NT can be interpreted as a natural raise of partner's notrump call.

South	North
1 ♡	2 ◇
2 NT	4 NT

Here 4 NT, a direct raise of partner's limit bid of 2 NT, is natural.

However, a *jump* to 4 NT over a suit call, and 4 NT by a player who has forced, are always conventional. In these sequences the assumption is that the 4 NT bidder knows where he is going.

3. When a player who has made a natural bid in notrumps makes a minimum bid of 4 NT in response to his partner's advance.

South	North
1 ♠	2 ◇
3 NT	4 ♣
4 NT	

South's 4 NT means that he has shown his values and is not prepared at this stage to respond to the slam suggestion.

REBIDS BY OPENER

A rebid of 1 NT is for many players related to the strength required for an opening 1 NT. When 1 NT is 12–14 a rebid of 1 NT indicates 15–16 points. When 1 NT is 15–17 a rebid of 1 NT indicates a weaker balanced hand. For a conventional arrangement after the rebid of 1 NT, see *Crowhurst Convention*.

A rebid of 2 NT over a response at the range of one shows about 17 or 18 in *Acol*, 19 or 20 points in Standard American. Practice varies in respect of a rebid of 2 NT over a response at the two level. In some systems it indicates a minimum, but in *Acol* and Standard American it is a constructive rebid, suggesting about 15 to 17.

A rebid of 3 NT over a response at the range of one indicates about 19 to 21 points. However, some players have an understanding that a sequence such as 1 ♦–1 ♥–3 NT should be based on a strong minor suit; partner is warned not to return to hearts. Over a response at the range of two the rebid suggests about 17 to 19 points.

For strong rebids in a suit, see *Reverse Bid* and *Forcing Bid*.

REDOUBLE

As is mentioned under *Penalty Double*, the odds are weighted against a doubler in close situations. On the other hand, the odds favour a player who contemplates a redouble.

Suppose that the likely issue is between making the contract and going down one. Not vulnerable, the redouble of a game contract such as 4 ♠ will bring in an extra 240 if the contract is made and will cost only an extra 100 if it is down one. This represents odds of nearly 5 to 2 in favour. Vulnerable, the odds are not so good: 240 to 200, just short of 5 to 4 in favour.

At the slam level the odds in favour of the redoubler are still better. A redouble of 6 ♠ will bring in an extra 360, while if the contract is down one, not vulnerable, it will have cost only 100.

Special types of redouble are described under *SOS Redouble*. The significance of a redouble by third hand after a take-out double by second hand is described under *Take-out Double*.

RELAY BID

An artificial bid just one step above partner's last call is a relay. The negative 2 ♦ in response to an opening 2 ♣ is a familiar example. Some European systems make considerable use of relays, increasing the range of expression. As a rule, the strong hand uses the relay and the weak hand shows its distribution.

RESPONSES TO OPENING BIDS OF ONE

A suit response at the level of one has a wide range in all systems, with a minimum of about 6 points. There is no fixed maximum; but see *Jump Shift*. Responses at the level of two range from a minimum of 10 on comparatively balanced hands with a five-card suit to, exceptionally, about 7 with a long, rebiddable suit. In some systems the response at the two level promises at least one further bid, and in others the response is forcing to 2 NT.

For responses in notrumps, see *Notrump Responses to Suit Opening*, and for raises see *Double Raise of Suit Opening*.

RESPONSIVE DOUBLE

This occurs when partner doubles an opening bid and third hand raises the suit.

South	West	North	East
1 ♡	Dble	2 ♡	?

East holds:

♠J742   ♡542   ◇AJ83   ♣K10

If North had passed, East would have bid 2 ♠, but to bid 2 ♠ now in competition would not be enough, and 3 ♠ on so moderate a suit is not appealing. A double by East would be a take-out double in return, putting the ball back into partner's court. If West bids 2 ♠ East can raise, and if he bids 3 ♣ East can transfer to 3 ◇. Responsive doubles are widely played, usually to the level of 3 ♠.

REVERSE BID

A player is said to reverse when, at the level of two or higher, he bids a second suit of higher rank than his first, as in these sequences:

(1)	South	North	(2)	South	North
	1 ♡	2 ◇		1 ◇	2 ♣
	2 ♠			2 ◇	2 ♡

In (1) the reverse by opener after a response at the two level is forcing, and so is any reverse by the responder, as in (2). A reverse by opener after a response at the one level normally shows upwards of 16 points; the requirements after a response at the two level are slightly less, especially when a fit is held for partner's suit.

Because it implies similar strength, any new suit at the three level is loosely described as a 'three-level reverse':

(3) *South* *North* (4) *South* *North*
    1 ♠   2 ◇   1 ◇   1 ♡
    3 ♣   2 ◇   3 ♣

In each case the new suit at the three level is forcing.

RIPSTRA CONVENTION

This is similar to *Landy*, except that the player who overcalls 1 NT, instead of always bidding 2 ♣ for take-out, names his better minor, 2 ♣ or 2 ◇. The convention can be played with stress on the major suits, promising at least four cards in each major, or to denote a three-suiter with distribution such as 3–4–1–5.

See, also, the defensive systems listed under *Astro*.

ROMAN BLACKWOOD

This is a device to identify aces when responding to a *Blackwood* 4 NT. Responder with one ace bids 5 ◇; with two aces of the same colour, 5 ♡; with two of the same rank, 5 ♠; with two of the odd combinations, 5 NT. The mnemonic, CRO, for colour, rank, odd, assists the forgetful.

Roman Blackwood is not widely played nowadays, for a sound technical reason: a player most needs to identify aces when he himself holds a void, and a player holding a void should as a rule not employ Blackwood.

ROMAN JUMP OVERCALLS

Jump overcalls in the *Roman System* show two-suited hands. The suits are always the suit named and the next higher suit, excluding the suit which has been opened by the opponent. Thus, over an opening bid of 1 ◇, an overcall of

2 ♡ shows hearts and spades.
2 ♠ shows spades and clubs.
3 ♣ shows clubs and hearts.

The strength shown is about that of a sound opening bid, though of course the respective vulnerability has a bearing. Very strong two-suiters are shown by a conventional overcall of 2 NT. Some players of other systems have adopted this style of jump overcall.

ROMAN SYSTEM

This system is not widely played nowadays, but in the hands especially of the Italian pair, Belladonna and Avarelli, it was extremely effective. These are the main opening sequences:

1 ♣: Usually a limited balanced hand in the 12–16 point range, but 1 ♣ serves also for hands in the 17–20 range containing four clubs and a five-card suit, for a balanced 21–22, and for unbalanced hands of game-going quality. The nature of the rebid—whether a minimum bid or a jump—indicates the type. The negative response to 1 ♣ is 1 ◇ and 1 NT is game-forcing.

1 ◇, 1 ♡ and 1 ♠: The hand must contain a five-card suit, but the opening may be in a shorter suit, the system relying heavily on the *Canapé* method. These openings are forcing and a one-step response is negative. A response of 1 NT (except to 1 ♠) is constructive. A sequence such as 1 ◇–1 ♡–1 NT means that opener holds at least three diamonds and five hearts (the suit in which partner has responded artificially).

1 NT: 17–20 balanced.

2 ♣: A moderate three-suiter, normally 12–16.

2 ◇: A strong three-suiter, 17–20. See *Roman 2 ◇*.

2 ♡, 2 ♠: At least five cards in the suit named and at least four clubs.

2 NT: Balanced 23–24.

The Roman system has its own style of defensive overcalls. A simple overcall is strictly limited. Any hand in the 12–16 range may qualify for a take-out double, without need for preparedness; the responder to a take-out double, if third hand has not bid, indicates his *short* suit. A jump overcall denotes the suit bid and the suit above, excluding the opener's suit. An overcall of 2 NT shows a two-suiter in which the suits are not adjacent. Overcalls in an opponent's suit are natural. A jump overcall in the opponent's suit indicates a very strong two-suiter—a giant take-out double.

ROMAN 2 ◇

In the original *Roman System* the bid of 2 ◇ showed a powerful three-suiter, 17–20 points, but the range was often extended when the convention was adopted by players of other systems. The only forcing response is 2 NT and opener then indicates his *short* suit. Many variations have been introduced. Some players use the convention at two levels, 17–20 or 21–24, and some, over 2 NT, rebid in the suit *below* the short suit, gaining space. The Roman 2 ◇ is effective when it can be used, but the incidence is rare and most tournament players have abandoned it in favour of the *Multi-coloured 2* ◇ or the semi-three-suiter of the *Precision System*.

ROMEX SYSTEM

In this system, devised by Dr George Rosenkranz of Mexico City, 2 ♣ is game-forcing, 2 ◇ indicates a balanced 19–20 points, 1 NT is either a balanced 21–22 or a strong unbalanced hand.

Balanced hands of limited strength are expressed by rebids in notrumps at minimum level. The system uses five-card majors with a forcing 1 NT response and has many specialized asking bids.

ROTH-STONE SYSTEM

This system is now rarely played in its entirety, but it was a pioneer in many important areas, notably five-card majors in first or second hand, with 1 NT as a forcing response; negative doubles; weak two-bids; unusual notrump; and weak jump overcalls. Other features are strong opening bids in first and second hand, with a single raise of a major forcing for one round, simple overcalls strong (compare *Baron System*). The system relies heavily on the slow approach method, and many jumps that would be forcing in other systems are weak bids.

RULE OF TWO AND THREE

This is a test whereby a player may judge how much he may reasonably risk when making a pre-emptive opening or a defensive overcall. The rule states that, vulnerable, a player can afford to overbid by two tricks; not vulnerable, by three tricks. For example:

♠x ♡KQJ9xxx ◇xx ♣QJ10

This hand contains probably seven playing tricks in a heart contract. Not vulnerable, it would be a fair risk to open 4 ♡, overbidding by three tricks; vulnerable, 3 ♡ would be enough.

The Rule is also called the Rule of 500 since, broadly speaking, it is fair to go down 500 to save a game.

SHARPLES DEFENCE TO 1 NT

This system of defence to 1 NT is similar in outline to *Ripstra*. An overcall of 2 ♣ signifies that the clubs are longer than the diamonds, an overcall of 2 ◇ signifies that the diamonds are longer than the clubs. The hand will always contain good support for spades and at least tolerance for hearts.

The only forcing response to the overcall is 2 NT. This requires partner to bid his suits 'upwards'. The bidding may stop in 4 ♣ or 4 ◇ if no major-suit fit is disclosed.

A direct jump to 3 NT over 2 ♣ or 2 ◇ is 'to play'. It will generally be based on a long minor, with the assurance of some fit in the hand of the overcaller.

See, also, the defensive systems listed under *Astro*.

SHARPLES 4 ♣

This convention is aimed at reaching delicate slams in a minor suit after a 1 NT opening and a *Stayman* response:

South	North
1 NT	2 ♣
2 ◇	?

♠KQ32　♡AJ9　◇K4　♣Q1083

6 ♣ may well be the best contract if North has four clubs. Playing Sharples, North bids 4 ♣, showing specifically a four-card suit. If South cannot co-operate, he may sign off in 4 NT; otherwise he may raise clubs or make an advance cue bid.

A jump to 4 ◇ after a Stayman sequence, has the same sense of proposing a slam in diamonds.

SHORT CLUB

A short club (or 'prepared' club) is an opening bid on a suit of less than four cards. In standard bidding it is sometimes a means of avoiding a rebid problem. For example:

♠A Q x x ♡Q 10 x ◇J x x ♣A J x

This hand is not strong enough for a standard 1 NT opening and the objection to 1 ♠ is that the player would have no sound rebid over a response in a new suit at the two level. The solution is to open with a bid in the three-card club suit. A short club may also be opened when the four-card major is unbiddable. Most players, having opened 1 ♣ on the hand above, would rebid 1 NT rather than 1 ♠ over a response of 1 ♠ or 1 ♡.

In systems that require five cards for a major-suit opening, pre-pared openings are very frequent. It is usual to open the better minor, whether clubs or diamonds.

SHORT-SUIT GAME TRIES

After a sequence such as 1 ♠–2 ♠, an opener who plays 'short suit trial bids' indicates his *shortest* side suit, usually a singleton. The theory is that this is more helpful than naming a second suit of three or four cards. Opposite a short-suit game try, a holding such as x x x or x x x x is a 'good' fit, whereas K J x x would suggest wasted values.

SIGN-OFF BID

A player is said to sign off when he makes a series of limited bids in response to his partner's forward moves, as in this sequence:

South	North
1 ♣	1 ♡
2 ♣	2 ♠
3 ♣	

South's 3 ♣ is a sign-off, denying the ability to bid notrumps or support either of his partner's suits.

In many situations a single bid can be interpreted as discouraging. For example, since there are many ways of advancing over a no-trump opening, a sequence such as 1 NT–2 ♡, if not a transfer bid, is a sign-off for most players.

SNAP

The initials stand for Strong Notrump After Passing. A response of
1 NT by a passed hand denotes 9 to 12 points, fairly balanced. The
scheme has the advantage of enabling partners with a combined
count in the range of 20 to 23 to play many hands in 1 NT that would
otherwise be thrown in or played at the two level. A disadvantage is
that responder with 6 to 8 points has a problem when partner opens
a major suit.

When SNAP is played, 2 NT becomes an idle response. It can
serve as a relatively balanced raise of partner's suit.

SOS REDOUBLE

The majority of redoubles in the part-score area are a cry for help,
not a gesture of confidence. We look first at a sequence where the
redouble is *not* for rescue.

South	West	North	East
1 ♠	Pass	Pass	Dble
Rdble			

Here South is redoubling a bid of his own before his partner has
passed the double. This shows strength.

A player who redoubles his own bid, certainly up to the level of
2 ♠, *when partner has passed the double* is asking to be rescued.

South	West	North	East
1 ♣	Dble	Pass	Pass
Rdble			

South	West	North	East
1 ♠	1 NT	Dble	Pass
Pass	Rdble		

These redoubles are SOS.

For many tournament players a redouble by a player whose
partner has been doubled in a low part score is also SOS:

South	West	North	East
1 ♡	2 ♣	Dble	Rdble

If East were content with 2 ♣ doubled he would pass, so his
redouble says 'Try something else'. It is sometimes possible to find a

haven in the suit bid by the opponents. This interpretation of the double is conventional and sometimes known as 'Kock-Werner', after the Swedish players who first suggested it.

SPLINTER BID

An unusual jump—one level higher than is needed for a force—denotes a singleton or void in the suit in which the jump is made, and shows strong support for partner's last suit. These are examples:

South	North
1 ◇	1 ♡
1 ♠	4 ♣

South	North
1 ♡	1 ♠
4 ◇	

Compare *Fragment Bid.*

SPUTNIK

See *Negative Double.*

STAYMAN CONVENTION

This well-known convention is named after the American expert, Sam Stayman, though he was not the first to propose the use of 2 ♣ as a conventional response to 1 NT. The primary object is to identify a 4–4 fit in a major. Over the 2 ♣ response the notrump opener rebids 2 ◇ with no four-card major, 2 ♡ with four hearts (also with four of each major), 2 ♠ with four spades.

When a strong notrump is played, and particularly in Standard American, the 2 ♣ response is often treated as constructive and opener with a maximum may rebid 2 NT. Similarly, a sequence such as 1 NT–2 ♣–2 ◇–2 ♡ invites a continuation. Another style is to play 2 ♣ as non-forcing, 2 ◇ as forcing Stayman.

When a weak notrump is played, 2 ♣ may be part of a rescue manoeuvre designed to avert a penalty double, and in this case the opener must never, on his first rebid, progress beyond 2 ♠.

There are also differences of practice when the responder continues with a new suit at the three level:

South	North
1 NT	2 ♣
2 any	3 ♠

Some players (irrespective of the strength of the notrump opening) treat the three-level bid as invitational, others as forcing.

2 ♣ followed by 3 ♣, in a sequence such as 1 NT–2 ♣–2 any–3 ♣, normally indicates a weak hand with long clubs. But here again some players, in accordance with the *Principle of Fast Arrival*, treat 1 NT–3 ♣ as weak, the more gradual approach as forcing.

Stayman with transfers

In a variation proposed by Kit Woolsey, called 'Puppet Stayman', the transfer principle is invoked. Opener may rebid in a five-card major or six-card minor, but in general he rebids 2 ◇. Now responder bids 2 ♡ with four spades, 2 ♠ with four hearts, 2 NT or (stronger) 3 NT with 4–4 in the majors. This style has two advantages: the opener's distributional features are more likely to be concealed, and the notrump opener is more likely to become the eventual declarer.

Stayman at a part score

At rubber bridge 2 ♣ at a part score retains its Stayman quality.

2 ♣ when 1 NT has been doubled

After 1 NT has been doubled by second hand, 2 ♣ by responder is assumed to be natural, though often it is a precursor to an SOS redouble.

Stayman by the defending side

There is less general agreement about the meaning of 2 ♣ in this type of sequence:

South	West	North	East
1 ◇	1 NT	Pass	2 ♣

The best arrangement here is to play 2 ♣ as natural, 2 ◇ as a request for a major.

TAKE-OUT DOUBLE

The usual formula to distinguish a take-out from a penalty double is this:

If partner has made a bid of any kind, then a double is a penalty double made with the expectation of defeating the contract.

If partner has not made a bid, a double of one or two in a suit is for take-out if made at the first opportunity of doubling.

The following sequences illustrate apparent exceptions or 'grey areas':

(1)	*South*	*West*	*North*	*East*
	1 ♥	Pass	3 ♥	<u>Dble</u>

Since East is more likely to wish to contest than to be doubling for penalties, this double at the three level, when only one suit has been named, is for take-out, though it should contain defensive tricks also.

(2)	*South*	*West*	*North*	*East*
	1 ♥	Pass	Pass	Dble
	Pass	Pass	2 ♣	<u>Dble</u>

East's second double is for penalties because although West has not made a positive bid his penalty pass on the previous round shows where his values lie.

(3)	*South*	*West*	*North*	*East*
	1 ♦	Pass	1 ♥	Pass
	2 ♥	Pass	Pass	<u>Dble</u>

East is not doubling hearts at the first opportunity, but he is in the balancing position and the opponents are evidently limited; this is a take-out double.

(4)	*South*	*West*	*North*	*East*
	1 ♦	Pass	1NT	Pass
	2 ♦	<u>Dble</u>		

On the surface there are two possible interpretations of West's double. He might have made a trap pass over 1 ♦ and be doubling now for penalties; or he might hold length in both majors and have been under strength for a double on the first round. This is a situation where experienced players would 'have it both ways': they would assume that partner, from his own holding, would be able to distinguish between the two possibilities. Note, however, that if North had responded 1 ♡ or 1 ♠, instead of limiting his hand with 1 NT, West's double would certainly have been for penalties, based on strong diamonds.

Requirements for a take-out double

In standard systems a take-out double by the second player promises the strength of an opening bid, together with preparedness for any response. The high-card strength may be slightly shaded when there is good support for both majors. When weak jump overcalls are played, there may be no alternative to a double on a fairly strong one-suited hand.

Responses to a take-out double

A jump response to a take-out double suggests about 8 to 10 points and is not forcing. The only forcing response is a bid of the opponent's suit.

A response of 1 NT is regarded by some players as constructive. This may be right in response to a double of a minor suit, but there may be no sensible alternative when responding to a double of a major suit on a weak hand.

The use of 2 ♣ as a conventional weakness response has gone out of fashion. For a weak response in the next suit, see *Herbert Convention*, and for a response in the short suit see *Roman System*.

Action by third hand over a double

After a take-out double by second hand, the traditional practice is to treat all changes of suit as non-forcing and to redouble on good hands, whether or not they contain support for partner's suit. Raises are pre-emptive and 2 NT indicates a 'sound' raise to three.

Some players consider that a better method is to respond in a new suit over the double on the same lines as though there had been no interference. A redouble is then specifically penalty-oriented, promising at least three cards in all suits other than the suit opened.

Subsequent cue bid by opener

There is no universal agreement about the meaning of a subsequent cue bid by the opener in this type of sequence:

South	West	North	East
1 ◇	Dble	Pass	1 ♡
Pass	2 ◇		

The idea that this should indicate strong diamonds has been abandoned. Most players would say that West's 2 ◇ was a forward-going move, asking partner for further description. West may be intending to support hearts, but he may also intend to take different action on the next round.

TEXAS CONVENTION

The original form of the Texas convention was as a transfer response at the four level after an opening 1 NT or 2 NT. A response of 4 ♣ was a transfer to 4 ♡, and 4 ◇ a transfer to 4 ♠. The main advantage was that the contract would be played by the notrump opener.

The prevalence of *Transfer Bids* at a lower level has made this type of response unnecessary, but Texas remains a lively force in the form of opening bids of 4 ♣ and 4 ◇, to distinguish between pre-emptive openings of 4 ♡ or 4 ♠ and somewhat stronger hands, not far short of an *Acol* two bid. Thus the dealer at game all might open 4 ◇ on:

♠ K Q J 10 8 4 2   ♡ 6 3   ◇ A Q J   ♣ 5

A responder who sees slam chances may bid the intermediate suit—in this case 4 ♡—without reference to his holding in that suit. On the hand above, the opener, with only one ace, would not at this stage accept the slam suggestion.

THIRD-HAND OPENING

The term implies an opening bid on a hand of less than normal strength, made to attract a lead or to impede the opposition.

♠ K Q 10 7 4   ♡ 5 3   ◇ A 8 4 2   ♣ 6 3

This would not be a sound opening first or second in hand, but in third position a sub-minimum bid of 1 ♠ is a reasonable risk, especially if not vulnerable.

THREE BID

See *Pre-emptive Bid.*

THREE NOTRUMP OPENING

A balanced 25 or 26 points can well be described by opening with an artificial 2 ♣ and rebidding 3 NT. It is common practice, therefore, to open 3 NT on a long, solid minor suit, with little or no outside strength. This is sometimes called the 'Gambling 3 NT'; the term is inappropriate because partner knows what is happening. This is a typical hand:

♠4   ♡952   ◇103   ♣AKQJ752

When the bid is made by the first or second player, partner will assume that at most one queen may be held outside the minor suit. This enables him to decide whether to stand 3 NT or take out.

If responder decides to play in opener's minor, he bids 4 ♣, and opener either passes or converts to 4 ◇.

When responder is interested in a slam, he may (by arrangement) bid 4 ◇ over 3 NT to ask opener to show a singleton. The replies are as follows:

4 ♡ shows a singleton or void in hearts.
4 ♠ shows a singleton or void in spades.
4 NT shows a hand containing no singleton or void.
5 ♣ or 5 ◇ shows a singleton or void in the other minor suit.

THREE NOTRUMP TAKE-OUT

One of the earliest systems of defence against opening three-bids was to double for penalties and bid 3 NT for take-out. 3 NT for take-out over a minor suit is clearly uneconomical. A playable method that combines various styles is to double 3 ♣ for take-out; to bid 3 ◇ over 3 ♣ for take-out; and to bid 3 NT for take-out over the majors. This method is sometimes called x–3–x, signifying double, 3 ◇, double.

TRANSFER BIDS

Transfer responses to an opening 1 NT, which contain many advantages, are very common in the tournament world. This is the usual scheme:

2 ♣ remains *Stayman.*
2 ♢ is a transfer to 2 ♡.
2 ♡ is a transfer to 2 ♠.
2 ♠ is a transfer to 2 NT.

2 NT is played as a transfer to 3 ♣. If followed by 3 NT it denotes a minor two-suiter. A transfer from 3 ♣ to 3 ♢ is weak.

For players who use a weak notrump, often sub-minimum in pairs at favourable vulnerability, there is advantage in playing 2 ♠ as a 'strong raise', meaning 'we should be in game if your opening is sound.' With a normal raise responder may bid 2 ♣ (irrespective of his major suits) and follow with 2 NT.

These transfer responses should not, in general, be used on very weak hands. An opener who has good support for the designated suit is not obliged to rebid at minimum level. For example, after 1NT–2 ♢, an opener who is maximum and has three hearts to an honour may rebid 2NT; with four hearts he may rebid 3 ♡.

When transfer responses are in use, direct responses at the three-level are not forcing; they may be played as pre-emptive or, more sensibly, as invitational, with a long suit.

Transfers over 2 NT

Transfer responses over 2 NT are also common. Again, 3 ♣ is Stayman (or *Baron*), 3 ♢ and 3 ♡ are transfers to 3 ♡ or 3 ♠, and 3 ♠ denotes interest in at least one minor. After a sequence such as 2 NT–3 ♡ opener has these options: with average values, 3 ♠; with a good hand for spades but only three trumps, 3 NT; with four trumps but only average controls, 4 ♠; with four trumps and good controls, a cue bid in a new suit.

After 2 NT–3 ♠ an opener whose main strength is in the majors will rebid 3 NT. If he is weak in one major he may rebid 4 ♣, to discover partner's intentions; and other conventional bids are available when he is strong in one or both minors.

Another idea is to play 2 NT–3 ♠ to denote 4–5 in the majors.

For other types of transfer bid, see *Flint Convention* and *Texas Convention.*

TRAP PASS

A player with good values who passes an opening bid on his right in the hope that opponents will get out of their depth is said to make a trap pass. The reputation of this manoeuvre has slumped since the early days of bridge, partly because players have learned to recognize misfits.

TRIAL BID

The usual occasion for a trial bid is after a single raise in a major. A bid in a new suit will then be a try for game. For example:

South	North
1 ♠	2 ♠
3 ◇	

South's 3 ◇ is a trial bid. It is forcing and does not put forward diamonds as an alternative contract. In judging his action, whether to sign off in 3 ♠ or go to game, responder will be influenced by his holding in diamonds. Generally speaking, a high honour or a singleton with four trumps constitutes a good fit.

See also *Short-Suit Game Tries.*

TRUMP ASKING BIDS

See *Grand Slam Force.*

TWO-CLUB OPENING

An opening of 2 ♣ may have various meanings, of which these are the most frequent:
1. Natural and game-forcing, as in the *Forcing Two-Bids.* This style is seldom encountered in the tournament world.
2. Conventional and strong. In systems that also use strong two-bids, such as *Acol*, 2 ♣ will always be a hand of quality, containing upwards of $4\frac{1}{2}$ honour tricks. In Acol a rebid of 2 NT, after the negative response of 2 ◇, suggests 23 or 24 points and is not forcing. In systems that use weak two-bids, 2 ♣ may be bid on various powerful hands of game-going strength.
3. In systems that use a strong 1 ♣ opening, such as *Precision*, 2 ♣

normally indicates a six-card suit in the range of 12 to 15. When only five clubs are held, 1 NT or 1 ◇ will usually be preferred.

4. In the *Roman System* 2 ♣ originally showed a moderate three-suiter, but some Roman players use the bid instead to show long clubs.

TWO-DIAMOND OPENING

An opening 2 ◇ has become the plaything of the theorists. In *Goren* and *Acol* the bid is natural and strong. For conventional uses, see *Benjamin Convention*, *Multicoloured 2 ◇*, *Precision System*, *Roman System*, and *Romex*.

TWO NOTRUMP OPENING

In systems that do not possess a strong conventional opening, usually 2 ♣, 2 NT suggests a balanced hand in the 22 to 24 points range. In systems where 2 ♣ is conventional, the range for 2 NT is 21–22, stronger hands being expressed by the sequence 2 ♣–2 ◇–2 NT.

Responses to 2 NT

A jump to four in a major suit is generally played as a sign-off, so that a sequence such as 2 NT–2 ♡–3 NT–4 ♡ contains a mild slam suggestion.

A response of 3 ♣ is sometimes played as *Stayman*, asking for the major suits, sometimes as *Baron*, asking for four-card suits 'upwards'. In this case a rebid of 3 NT implies four (or five) clubs.

UNASSUMING CUE BIDS

The range and accuracy of bids and raises by the defending side can be much improved by extended use of cue bids.

South	West	North	East
1 ♣	1 ♠	Pass	2 ♣

South	West	North	East
1 ◇	1 ♡	2 ◇	3 ◇

In each case the traditional meaning of East's bid of the opponent's suit is that he has game-going values, probably with strong support for partner. When 'unassuming cue bids' (first classified in *Bridge for Tournament Players*) are employed, East's bid denotes a sound, as opposed to a mainly defensive, raise of partner's overcall. East may make the same call on very strong hands as well.

An important advantage is that when the overcaller's partner raises the suit directly, to whatever level, his raise is known to be based on distributional rather than high-card strength.

UNPENALTY DOUBLES

Unpenalty doubles are a conventional arrangement, designed to improve partnership co-operation when there is a question whether or not to sacrifice against a slam. They arise only when the weaker side has bid and supported a suit. Say that the bidding goes:

South	West	North	East
1 ♠	2 ◇	2 ♡	3 ◇
4 NT	Pass	5 ◇	Pass
6 ♡	?		

At this point West, holding 0 or 2 likely defensive tricks, will pass. If East holds not more than one defensive trick he will double and West will sacrifice or pass.

If instead West holds one likely defensive trick, he will double 6 ♡. East, holding no defensive trick, will sacrifice.

At I.M.P. it is usual to play unpenalty doubles only when not vulnerable. At Pairs (where to lose 1,400 against 1,430 may be a minor triumph) unpenalty doubles may be played at game all as well.

UNUSUAL NOTRUMP

When a bid in notrumps cannot be genuine, it is conventionally described as 'unusual' and indicates distributional values in the minor suits or, if a minor suit has been bid, in the two lowest-ranking unbid suits. These are some sequences where doubt may exist:

(1)	South	West	North	East
	1 ◇	2 NT		

Though in logic the overcall could be genuine, it is by custom treated as 'unusual', promising in this instance at least 5–5 in hearts and clubs.

(2)	South	West	North	East
	1 ♡	Pass	Pass	2 NT

Here East's 2 NT may be based on a good minor suit, but the bid is in essence natural.

(3)

South	West	North	East
Pass	1 ♦	Pass	1 ♠
<u>1 NT</u>			

Unusual, because South would not intervene on a balanced hand that did not justify an opening bid. A second-round double would similarly indicate hearts and clubs, but 1 NT stresses distributional assets.

(4)

South	West	North	East
Pass	Pass	1 ♦	Pass
1 ♠	Pass	Pass	<u>1 NT</u>

East is in the protective or balancing position and his 1 NT is natural.

(5)

South	West	North	East
1 ♡	Pass	2 ♦	<u>2 NT</u>

Unusual, because it is more or less impossible for East to have the values for a natural 2 NT when one opponent has opened and the other has responded at the level of two. East is marked with a black two-suiter, the clubs probably longer than the spades.

(6)

South	West	North	East
1 ♠	2 ♣	2 ♠	Pass
Pass	<u>2 NT</u>		

West's 2 NT can hardly be natural, since he made a simple overcall on the previous round. He is showing length in clubs and diamonds. In the following sequence the same kind of message is expressed by the player who has opened the bidding:

(7)

South	West	North	East
1 ♦	1 ♠	Pass	3 ♠
<u>3 NT</u>			

South's 3 NT can hardly be natural. If he had a minor two-suiter he would be able to contest now with 4 ♣. The presumption in this case is that he has the red suits, probably five hearts and six diamonds.

In *The Acol System of Bidding* the present authors concluded their review of the unusual notrump with this *caveat*:

'A point to bear in mind about the unusual notrump is that if opponents eventually buy the contract the declarer will have a valuable guide to the distribution of the unseen hands. It is therefore unwise to brandish this toy except when you have a definite possibility of challenging for the contract. At game to North-South the bidding goes:

South	West	North	East
1 ♡	Pass	1 ♠	?

'East holds:

♠5   ♡52   ◇KJ863   ♣A8642

'It is absurd to come in with 2 NT (or, indeed, to overcall an opening bid with 2 NT) on these values. If opponents have a misfit they will play for a penalty, and if instead they win the contract either in a suit or notrumps they will benefit considerably from the knowledge that one defender holds ten cards in the minor suits.'

VIENNA SYSTEM

This system, played by Austrian world champions in the 1930s, is seldom encountered nowadays, but some of its features are discernible in other systems. An opening 1 ♣ in Vienna denotes a limited hand with no 5-card suit. In response, 1 ◇ is negative and 1 NT is game-forcing. An opening 1 NT denotes at least 17 and may be bid with any distribution; it is forcing for one round. Opening bids of 1 ◇, 1 ♡ and 1 ♠ show 11–17 points and at least a 5-card suit.

WEAK JUMP OVERCALL

A jump overcall may be used as a pre-emptive measure in such a sequence as this:

South	West	North	East
		1 ◇	2 ♡ (or 2 ♠ or 3 ♣)

The overcall suggests the equivalent of a weak two-bid: 6 to 11 points and a six-card suit. Vulnerability naturally has a bearing.

The jump remains weak when both opponents have spoken, as in this sequence:

South	West	North	East
1 ♢	Pass	1 ♡	2 ♠ (or 3 ♣)

Weak jump overcalls are standard practice in America, but less common elsewhere.

Some partnerships abandon the weak jump overcall when the overcaller is vulnerable and the opponents are not.

WEAK NOTRUMP

A weak notrump normally has a range of 12–13, or 12–14 points. A *Mini-notrump*, favoured by some players in certain situations, is normally 10–12. A *rebid* of 1 NT, by a player whose system includes a weak notrump opening, suggests 15–16 points, but see *Crowhurst Convention*.

WEAK TWO-BID

In systems that have 2 ♣ or 1 ♣ as a strong artificial opening, it is common to use openings of 2 ♡ and 2 ♠ as mild pre-emptive manoeuvres.

The usual requirements for a weak two-bid are: a six-card suit headed by at least the Q J 10; 6 to 11 points in high cards with, usually, $1\frac{1}{2}$ or 2 quick tricks; five or six likely playing tricks, according to vulnerability; little or no support for the other major suit. This is a typical 2 ♡ opening:

♠ 8 3   ♡ A Q J 7 5 3   ♢ 9 2   ♣ Q 10 6

Responding to weak two-bids

A response of 2 NT is a one-round force, suggesting at least the equivalent of opening values. Opener may show a minimum by rebidding his own suit or, by arrangement, by rebidding 3 ♣. A rebid in another suit is constructive and shows a feature rather than a biddable suit. For a conventional system of rebids, see *Ogust Rebids*.

A single raise of a weak two is generally treated as pre-emptive. Practice differs in respect of a response in a new suit: some play it as constructive but not forcing, others as denying support for opener's suit and suggesting an alternative contract.

Defence to weak two-bids

The simplest defence is to play a double for take-out and 2 NT to show a guard in the enemy suit, as when overcalling a bid of one. Alternatively, it is possible to enlist the same kind of defence that the partners use against three-bids—conventions such as *Fishbein* or *Lower Minor*.

Part 2

PLAY

ACE FROM ACE-KING

For players who follow standard practice in leading the queen from
Q J, K from K Q, it is in a sense logical to lead the ace from a
combination headed by A K. Most tournament players do so. The
traditional lead of the king from A K can create a problem for a
partner who holds J x x and cannot interpret the lead with confidence. On the other hand, if the conventional lead from A K is the
ace, a player wishing to lead an unsupported ace runs the risk of
misleading his partner.

An alternative idea, propounded by the Norwegian writer, Helge
Vinje, is to lead the ace from an even-numbered suit (A K x x or
A K x x x x), the king from an odd-numbered suit (A K x or
A K x x x).

ANTI-PERCENTAGE PLAY

A player who needs a swing on the last board of a match, or a top in a
pairs, may decide to make an anti-percentage play. For example,
with ten cards of a suit, missing the king, he may play for the drop
instead of finessing. By so doing he plays against the field and may
obtain an excellent result if his luck is in.

ASSUMPTION

In the course of play the declarer may need to make certain assumptions about the unseen hands. When the contract cannot be made
unless the cards lie in a certain fashion, he assumes that they do lie in
that way. Conversely, when the contract will be safe unless the cards
are badly placed, declarer assumes that they are so placed and
considers what can be done about it.

Every player makes use of assumption in some degree. Sometimes declarer knows he must play for a 3–3 break in a critical suit (a
favourable assumption), sometimes he can allow for a 4–2 break.
This is a less familiar example of a favourable assumption:

♠A 4 2
♡K Q
◇8 7
♣Q J 10 7 6 4

♠K 6 3
♡J 9 5 2
◇A K 4 2
♣5 2

The contract is 3 NT and West leads a low heart, the king winning. It may seem natural to lead a club honour from dummy, but competent defenders will duck this trick. It will then be hard to bring in the suit.

Declarer must therefore make the favourable assumption that one defender holds a singleton ace or king. At the second trick he leads a low club from the table, and if the ace or the king comes up he will have no more problems.

Second-degree assumption

What is known as 'second-degree assumption' is a particularly interesting extension. Suppose the contract cannot be made unless a certain card is favourably placed. In that case declarer should assume that it is so placed. At the same time he should consider what follows from that. He may be led to a further assumption concerning another suit. This would be *second-degree assumption*. A standard example:

♠ Q 4 3 2
♡ K J 2
♢ A Q J
♣ 9 5 2

♠ K 8 7 6 5
♡ A Q 6
♢ 10 7 4
♣ J 4

South is in 4 ♠ and West leads king, ace and another club. On ruffing East's queen, how should South play trumps?

South must make the favourable assumption that West holds ♢ K, for otherwise the contract must fail. In that case West, who has already shown up with ♣ A K, is unlikely to hold ♠ A. South therefore makes the second-degree assumption that East holds this card. He crosses to dummy with a heart and leads a low spade from the table, because the ace may be singleton.

In the next example declarer starts by making an unfavourable assumption:

♠K Q 9 3
♡K J 8
♢6 2
♣K 10 7 6

♠A 10 8 7 5 4
♡7 3
♢Q 9 5
♣3 2

South	West	North	East
—	—	—	Pass
Pass	Pass	1 ♣	Pass
1 ♠	Pass	2 ♠	Pass
3 ♠	Pass	Pass	Pass

West leads a low diamond and East wins with the ace, returning the 3. West wins with the jack and switches to a low heart. If both heart honours are wrong the contract must fail, so the first necessary assumption is that East does not hold ♡A Q.

The next reflection is that the contract will be safe if West holds ♣A. So declarer must direct his mind to the situation where East holds ♣A and either ace or queen of hearts.

Next point: East passed as dealer, so will probably not hold three aces. Conclusion: go up with ♡K, playing East for ♣A and ♡Q.

Second-degree assumptions frequently concern distribution. When only a poor division of a certain suit will trouble declarer, this may have a bearing on the remaining suits.

♠A 10 7 2
♡Q 8
♢8 6 3 2
♣A Q 5

♠K Q 9 6
♡K 6
♢A Q J 4
♣K J 7

South is in 4 ♠ and West leads ♡J, which East wins with the ace. South wins the next heart and considers how to tackle trumps. The contract should be easy unless West holds ♢K 10 x x. Since he is mentally placing West with four diamonds, South should play East for possible length in spades, beginning with the king and following with a low spade to the ace.

ATTACKING LEAD

Against suit contracts, especially, a defender may think in terms of either an attacking or a passive opening lead. A lead from a strong combination of honours, such as the king from K Q J x, is ideal because it combines safety with attack. Even when no such combination is present, an attacking lead is indicated when there is evidence that the opponents have length and strength in a side suit. In this case the defenders cannot usually afford to play a safe game: they must aim to set up quick tricks in the remaining suits. In general, a lead from a relatively short suit such as K x x is better attack than from a longer suit such as Q x x x x.

ATTITUDE SIGNALS

This is the vogue word for a signal expressing encouragement or discouragement rather than 'count' (odd number of cards or even). Suppose that a queen is led and partner holds the 6 and 3: the attitude signal is the 3, the count signal the 6 (high-low with an even number). Whether, in a particular situation, a signal should be 'attitude' or 'count' depends on partnership understanding.

A different way to express 'attitude' is by playing an odd card to encourage, an even card to discourage—or the other way round!

Similarly, there are 'attitude leads'. The lower the spot card led against notrumps, the stronger the suggestion that the suit be returned. See *Buso* and *Journalist Leads*.

AUTOMATIC SQUEEZE

A squeeze is said to be automatic, as opposed to positional (or one-way), when it would be equally effective against either defender.

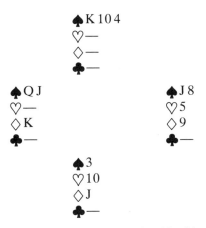

Playing in notrumps, South leads the 10 of hearts and squeezes West. The squeeze would work equally well if the East-West hands were interchanged.

The distinguishing feature of an automatic squeeze is that the one-card menace and the squeeze card are in the same hand, opposite the two-card menace. When the squeeze card is played, the discard from the opposite hand is 'automatic': it does not depend on the left-hand opponent's discard.

AVOIDANCE PLAY

This name can be given to any move that is aimed at keeping a particular defender out of the lead while the declarer establishes his tricks. It is an important branch of play, very common in notrump contracts.

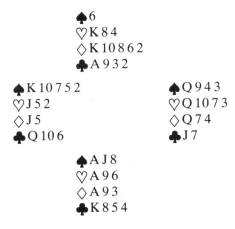

South is in 3 NT and West leads ♠5, South taking East's queen with the ace. As he must try to develop the diamonds without letting East in, South crosses to ◇K and leads a low diamond from dummy, intending to play the 9 if East follows low. This is an avoidance play.

In the following examples West is the player who is to be kept out:

(1)   6 5 3   (2)   1 0 8 6

  J 7 2   K 1 0   J 9 3   Q 7 2

     A Q 9 8 4   A K 5 4

In the first example declarer leads the suit from dummy. If East plays the king, South plays low. If East plays the 10, South finesses the queen and then crosses to dummy in another suit for the next lead; this time, when East's king appears, it is allowed to hold.

In the second example declarer denies West an entry by leading twice from dummy towards the A K. If East unblocks by playing the queen on the first or second round, he is allowed to hold the trick.

When tricks are needed in more than one suit, the need for avoidance may determine which should be tackled first:

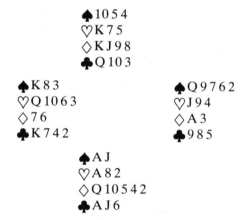

```
              ♠10 5 4
              ♡K 7 5
              ◇K J 9 8
              ♣Q 10 3
♠K 8 3                      ♠Q 9 7 6 2
♡Q 10 6 3                   ♡J 9 4
◇7 6                        ◇A 3
♣K 7 4 2                    ♣9 8 5
              ♠A J
              ♡A 8 2
              ◇Q 10 5 4 2
              ♣A J 6
```

The contract is 3 NT and West leads ♡3. South does not hold up, as he can afford to lose two heart tricks, a club and a diamond. However, if South begins by tackling diamonds, East may win and find the switch to a spade. As the cards lie, declarer then makes only eight tricks.

Here East is the dangerous opponent, as South does not fear a spade switch from West's side. South should therefore plan to avoid East by winning the first heart in dummy and leading ♣Q. West wins but can do no damage.

A distinctive type of avoidance occurs when declarer leads through an opponent's high card in circumstances where the defender can play this card only at the cost of a trick.

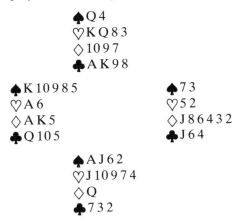

```
                    ♠Q4
                    ♡KQ83
                    ◇1097
                    ♣AK98
♠K10985                         ♠73
♡A6                             ♡52
◇AK5                            ◇J86432
♣Q105                           ♣J64
                    ♠AJ62
                    ♡J10974
                    ◇Q
                    ♣732
```

West opens 1♠, North doubles and South lands in 4♡. Diamonds are led and declarer ruffs the second round. He forces out ♡A and ruffs the diamond return but is faced with the danger of losing a trick in each of the black suits, as the spade finesse seems sure to fail.

The solution is to lead a low spade from the South hand, a form of avoidance. If West does not play the king, he will not make it, and if he does play it, two club losers from dummy will eventually go away on declarer's spades.

BACKWARD FINESSE

In some situations where a straight finesse would fail, the enemy honour can be picked up by an unusual type of finesse taken in the opposite direction.

```
            K64
Q73                     10852
            AJ9
```

A simple finesse of the jack would lose to the queen. Possession of the 9, however, enables South to execute a backward finesse. He can lead the jack and, if this is covered by the queen, he can finesse the 9 on the way back.

A backward finesse, as compared with a simple finesse, depends on two cards being favourably placed; in the example above, the queen and the 10. The manoeuvre is accordingly more common in defence, when a player can see from the dummy that a natural finesse would lose. In this example East initiates a finesse against the jack:

9 x x

Q x x   K 10 8 x

A J x

East is on lead and, seeing the 9 in dummy, leads the 10. Note that if the South hand happened to be the dummy, the 10 would still be the card to lead.

BATH COUP

This is a simple hold-up play by declarer when he has A J x and the king is led. It has the special advantage of forcing the defender to shift to another suit or concede a trick.

x x x

K Q 10 x   x x x

A J x

West leads the king and is allowed to hold the trick. South now has a major tenace and will win two tricks if West continues.

The play is the same in effect when the ace and jack are in different hands. Suppose North has A x x, West and East the same as before, and South J x x. Again South holds off when the king is led and West must either switch or concede a trick.

The play dates from the days of whist and is known as the Bath Coup from having first been executed in that city.

BENJAMIN TRUMP SIGNAL

This is a method of giving a count in a specified side suit by echoing or not echoing in trumps. It was suggested by Albert Benjamin in *Bridge Magazine*.

The highest unplayed side suit is described as the 'count suit'. When a defender echoes in trumps he shows an even number in the count suit, and when he does not echo he shows an odd number of cards in the count suit. This of course assumes that he has at least two expendable trumps.

For example, suppose spades are trumps, a heart is led, and declarer wins and plays trumps. In this situation the count suit will be diamonds.

This is one of the hands given by the author of the convention:

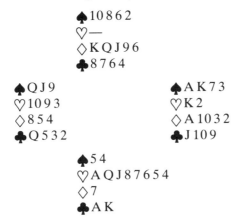

♠10 8 6 2
♡ —
◇K Q J 9 6
♣8 7 6 4

♠Q J 9
♡10 9 3
◇8 5 4
♣Q 5 3 2

♠A K 7 3
♡K 2
◇A 10 3 2
♣J 10 9

♠5 4
♡A Q J 8 7 6 5 4
◇7
♣A K

East opens 1 NT and South overcalls with 4 ♡, which is passed out. Spades are led and South ruffs the third round. He leads A Q of trumps and East, on winning with the king, returns the fourth spade to promote West's 10 of trumps. On this trick, however, declarer discards his losing diamond and claims the balance, failing by only one trick.

If East had cashed ◇A before leading the fourth trump the contract would have been set two tricks. However, in the absence of special signalling methods it would be risky for East to cash ◇A, as South might be void in diamonds, holding ♣A K Q perhaps. In that case West's ♡10 would not be promoted and the contract would be made.

Using the Benjamin Trump Signal, West follows low-high in trumps, showing an odd number of diamonds—the count suit. East may then safely cash ◇A before leading the fourth spade.

There is scope for alternative schemes when, for one reason or another, the count in the 'official' count suit is already known to the defenders.

Compare *Vinje Trump Signal.*

BLOCKING PLAY

This is the name for a group of manoeuvres aimed at preventing, or at any rate delaying, the run of an enemy suit. The common feature is that second hand plays high in circumstances where it is normal to play low. For example:

(1)	A 7	
K J 8 5 2		Q 6
	10 9 4 3	

In this well-known situation West, having overcalled in this suit, leads the 5 against a notrump contract. Reading the position, declarer goes up with dummy's ace on the opening lead. Now the defenders cannot run the suit directly they regain the lead. The blocking play will be especially effective if West has only one entry and this can be attacked at once. Again:

(2)	6 3		(3)	K 10 5	
Q 9 2		A 10 7 5 4	7 3		A J 9 6 2
	K J 8			Q 8 4	

In (2) West leads the 2 of a suit bid by his partner. East wins and returns the 5. Most defenders in East's position, holding A Q x x x, would play the queen on the opening lead. Therefore South may decide to go in with the king on the second round, leaving the suit blocked until West has cashed the queen and given partner the lead.

In (3) West leads the 7 and declarer, if he can read the position, should play the king from dummy. East wins but has to abandon the suit or give declarer a trick.

All blocking plays are equally available to both sides. Thus in the last example if West is the declarer and leads this suit, North should go in with the king to prevent declarer from finessing. If dummy has no outside entry, declarer is held to one trick.

In practical play the defenders in fact have more opportunity for blocking plays than the declarer. A different motive for blocking occurs in these examples:

(4)	Q 9 5 3		(5)	K Q 4	
10 8 6 2		7	9 8 5 3		J 7 2
	A K J 4			A 10 6	

In (4) declarer plays off the A K, then leads the 4. West sees that to put in the 10 cannot cost and will prevent declarer from gaining an extra entry to dummy by finessing the 9. In (5) declarer leads small from dummy intending to finesse the 10 for reasons of entry. By inserting the jack East prevents the entry-finesse.

BUSO

This term is used of the Italian style of leads against notrump contracts. The principle is that the lower the card led, the stronger the suggestion that this suit be returned. Thus a player holding ♠ A Q 10 7 and ♡ J 7 5 4 2 might lead the 5 of hearts; but with the same heart holding and 3–5–3–2 distribution, the lead might be the 2 of hearts. See *Attitude Signals*.

COMBINATION FINESSE

A combination finesse is played when the adverse honours include two cards of equal rank. Frequently the first finesse is expected not to win the trick but to prepare the ground for a second finesse in the same suit.

(1) A J 10	(2) A J 9
x x x	x x x

In (1) South leads low and finesses the 10. If it loses to the king or queen, he later takes a second finesse against the outstanding honour.

In (2) South begins with a deep finesse of the 9. If this draws the king or queen, there will be a simple finesse for the remaining high honour. This sequence of play gives a 37 per cent chance of two tricks. Finessing the jack on the first round would give only a 25 per cent chance. Again:

(3) A Q 9	(4) K 10 9
x x x	x x x

In (3), if South begins with a finesse of the 9, he has a 63 per cent chance of two tricks. In (4) a finesse of the 9 and then the 10 affords a 79 per cent chance of making at least one trick.

COMMUNICATION PLAY

Among the plays primarily concerned with establishing or cutting communications are the following: *Avoidance Play, Blocking Play, Deschapelles Coup, Ducking, Entry-Killing Play, Hold-up Play, Merrimac Coup, Scissors Coup* and *Unblocking Play.*

COUNTING THE HAND

A player is said to 'count the hand' when he works out the suit length in the unseen hands. A perfect count arises when there is a count of three suits and the distribution of the fourth suit can therefore be determined with certainty. For example:

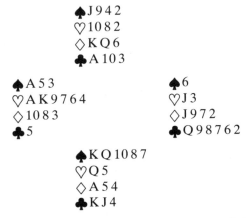

South plays in 4 ♠ after West has opened 1 ♡. The defence begins with three rounds of hearts, East ruffing and South over-ruffing. When trumps are led West wins the second round and exits with his last trump.

Declarer needs to find ♣ Q to make his contract. He already has a count of spades and hearts and should now play out the diamonds. When West follows to three rounds he is known to have started with at least three diamonds, six hearts and three spades. He cannot, therefore, hold more than one club, so declarer can ensure his contract by playing off dummy's ♣ A and finessing against East.

A partial count

When declarer has information about the layout of even one suit, this will have a bearing on the other suits. Suppose this is the trump suit:

(1)   K x   (2)   Q 10 x

A J 10 9 x x   K 9 8 7 x

In each case East has become marked by the bidding or the early play with length in another suit. In (1) South might abandon the normal percentage play and lead the jack for a first-round finesse. In (2) he would not lead up to the queen and then finesse for the jack on the way back, the normal play, but would lead the 9 and run it on the first round. This will gain in particular when West holds J x x x or A J x x.

COUP

This term may be applied to any unusual tactical stroke in the field of card play. The following coups have acquired distinctive titles: *Bath Coup, Coup de l'agonie, Coup en passant, Crocodile Coup, Deschapelles Coup, Devil's Coup, Grand Coup, Grosvenor Coup, Merrimac Coup, Scissors Coup, Trump Coup* and *Vienna Coup*.

COUP DE L'AGONIE

This French phrase describes a situation which is certainly most painful for a defender who has a trump holding such as A x x. Twice he ruffs low to prevent declarer from obtaining a critical discard, and next time he must either discard or part with his ace of trumps.

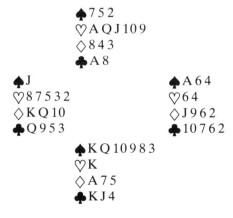

```
            ♠752
            ♡AQJ109
            ◇843
            ♣A8
♠J                        ♠A64
♡87532                    ♡64
◇KQ10                     ◇J962
♣Q953                     ♣10762
            ♠KQ10983
            ♡K
            ◇A75
            ♣KJ4
```

Playing in 6♠, South wins the diamond lead and sets out to discard his diamond losers on dummy's hearts. One diamond goes away on the second heart, but the third round is ruffed and over-ruffed. South crosses to ♣A and leads a fourth heart, which again is ruffed and over-ruffed. Declarer enters dummy again by ruffing the third round of clubs and leads a fifth heart, completing East's ordeal.

COUP EN PASSANT

This is a very useful manoeuvre in which declarer makes a low trump which would be a loser if a trump were led. This is the typical end position:

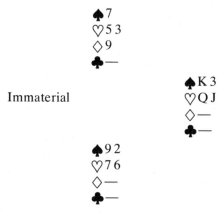

Hearts are trumps. Declarer plays the diamond from dummy and, whether East ruffs or not, must make a trump trick *en passant*. The position arises from the following deal:

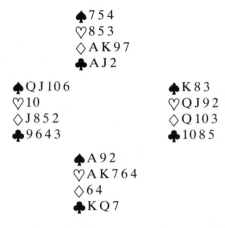

The contract is 4 ♡ and West leads ♠Q. South wins and lays down ♡A K. When West shows out, South appears to have four losers—two in trumps and two in spades. One of these is easily circumvented, however. South takes three rounds of diamonds, ruffing the third, then the three top clubs, reaching the required end position.

COVERING HONOURS

This is a difficult area of defensive play because what is right on one occasion may be wrong on another. Thus, compare these two situations:

(1)   A 10 8 5 3   (2)   A 10 8 5 3

  Q 4 2   K 9 6   Q 4 2   7 6

      J 7   K J 9

In each case the jack is led from South and West sees the same cards in dummy. In (1) he must cover, in (2) he does better not to cover—and this would apply with even more force if South held K J 9 x, as in this case he would probably play for the drop.

In so far as it is possible to lay down general rules, it is usually right to cover when two honour cards are visible on the left, as in (1) above. It is usually wrong to cover when you can see only one honour on your left and also when, sitting over the dummy, you can see two honours on your right. Thus:

(3)   A 7 5 3   (4)   J 10 2

  Q 6 4   K 9 8   K 9 8   Q 6 4

    J 10 2   A 7 5 3

In (3) the jack is led from South, in (4) from North, the dummy. In each case the defender, following the rule described above, should refrain from covering on the first round.

The decision is more difficult when there are two honours on your right and you hold a doubleton:

      (5)   Q J 9 3

      10 8 2   K 4

        A 7 6 5

Here it is better not to cover when the queen is led. If you play low, declarer will have a guess on the next round, whereas if you cover he is likely to finesse the 10 next time.

It is always wrong to cover when there is no chance that the play will promote a lower card in partner's hand or your own. This is an elementary example:

(6)   ♠J942

♠K   ♠Q75

♠A10863

South, who has opened 1 ♠, plays in 4 ♠. It would be singularly inept for East to cover dummy's jack with the queen.

CRASHING HONOURS

There are several artful ways in which a declarer may induce the defenders to crash their high cards on one another. As was remarked under the preceding title, *Covering Honours*, it is generally right for the second hand to cover the lead of an unsupported high card. Declarer can exploit that tendency in situations such as the following:

Q743

A   K5

J109862

Dummy leads the queen in the hope that East may cover.

More subtle examples of this kind of play occur when the declarer's honours are not in sequence:

Q952

107643

Suppose that declarer can judge that East has two or more cards in this suit. To lead dummy's queen cannot cost and may provoke East, holding K J x or A J x, to cover, telescoping the defenders' tricks.

A defender who is marked with length in the trump suit can often be subjected to psychological pressure of that kind:

J75

A   KQ93

108642

If East is marked with length in the suit it may gain to lead the jack. East may cover, thinking that declarer has A 10 8 x x and that to duck would lose a tempo. The same is true of the following situation:

J 6 5 4

Q   K 10 8 2

A 9 7 3

In the above examples the declarer has to able to infer that a particular defender has length in the suit. Otherwise the honour-crashing play may cost a trick. For instance, in the last example the lead of the jack would be a losing play if East held a singleton.

There is another group of plays in which the attempt to crash the honours is a 'free shot' that cannot cost. For example:

J 7

K   Q 10 9 3

A 8 6 5 4 2

Dummy leads the jack; if East covers, the defenders can be held to two tricks instead of three.

In a final example, dummy leads a high card but declarer has no intention of letting it run:

9 6 5 3

A K Q 7 2

Provided there are plentiful entries to the table, to lead the 9 is a subtlety that costs nothing. If East does not cover, declarer plays high. Once in a while, East will hold the outstanding four cards and may be persuaded to cover the 9. Then his J 10 8 4 can be picked up without loss.

CRISS-CROSS SQUEEZE

In this variation there is no two-card menace headed by a winner, as in other forms of squeeze. Instead there is an isolated winner in each hand, with two cards of lower rank lying opposite.

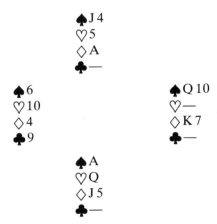

South leads ♡Q and East is squeezed. Whichever suit East unguards, declarer cashes the winner and crosses to the opposite hand to make the long card. A criss-cross squeeze is necessarily automatic.

CROCODILE COUP

The term describes a situation where a defender opens his jaws like a crocodile to swallow a card in his partner's hand which must not be allowed to win the trick. There was an example in the match between Germany and France in the 1979 European Championship:

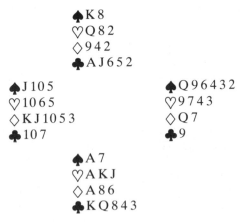

Playing in 6 ♣, South won the spade lead in dummy and at once led a diamond to the ace. This was clever play, since at this early stage the defenders might not realize the necessity to unblock. He then drew trumps (East again failing to disembarrass himself of ◇Q), eliminated the spades and hearts, and exited with a low diamond from hand. The German defender, von Gynz, now played the crocodile coup, going up with the king of diamonds so that his partner would not be left on play with the queen.

CROSSRUFF PLAY

A crossruff takes place when plain suits are ruffed alternately in the two hands. It is likely to be the best plan whenever declarer has a short suit in each hand and can see that he will fall short of his contract if he draws trumps.

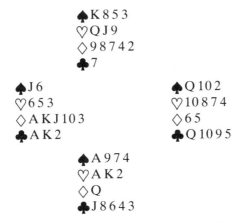

Dummy:
♠ K 8 5 3
♡ Q J 9
◇ 9 8 7 4 2
♣ 7

West:
♠ J 6
♡ 6 5 3
◇ A K J 10 3
♣ A K 2

East:
♠ Q 10 2
♡ 10 8 7 4
◇ 6 5
♣ Q 10 9 5

South:
♠ A 9 7 4
♡ A K 2
◇ Q
♣ J 8 6 4 3

South plays at 4 ♠ after West has opened 1 ◇. West begins with two top diamonds and South ruffs. A count of winners shows that the only hope is a crossruff.

The first move is to give up a club. If a trump is returned South wins in his hand and cashes three rounds of hearts. Then he cross-ruffs the minor suits. He makes seven tricks in spades and three in hearts.

Cashing the plain winners (unless they are needed for entries) before setting about the crossruff is an essential preliminary. Here, had South not cashed the hearts, East would have discarded hearts when declarer led diamonds from the table, and declarer would have been unable to cash his side winners.

DECEPTIVE LEAD

An unorthodox lead from an honour combination, such as the jack from Q J, when the queen would be conventional, is a common form of deception. The 9 from 10 9 or 10 9 x may be effective when the cards lie as follows:

(1)	Q 6 4	(2)	J 6 4	
10 9		J 3 2	10 9 3	K 2
	A K 8 7 5		A Q 8 7 5	

In 1, West leads the 9. If the declarer reads this as a true card, he may go up with dummy's queen and play East for J 10 3 2. The second example is a variation of the same play: on the lead of the 9 declarer may put up the jack, intending to play East for K 10 x. Left to himself, declarer might well make all five tricks.

The underlead of an ace against a suit contract, in the hope of finding dummy with a holding such as K J x, ranks as deceptive and is often made when the dummy is marked with strength. The underlead of an ace when dummy is marked with a void may also be a clever move.

There is often scope for deception when leading from a long suit against notrumps. A player who is strong all round may choose to lead, say, the 8 from A Q 8 6 2, to create the impression that he is leading 'top-of-nothing'. Alternatively, a fifth-best, instead of fourth-best, lead from a long suit may cause declarer to adopt an inferior line of play.

DEFENDING AGAINST SQUEEZES

Many squeezes can be defeated by an early attack on entries. This is especially true of squeezes that depend on a double menace with entries in each hand, such as K x x opposite A x x. In practical play a defender can often see that a squeeze is declarer's only hope and may not need to visualize the exact end position.

Defenders can sometimes prevent declarer from bringing about the position where he can win all the remaining tricks but one, a necessary condition for many squeezes. At notrumps, in particular, a defender should be cautious of cashing a long suit unless he has some idea of where the setting trick will come from.

Sometimes defenders can kill the menace cards needed for a squeeze by playing the suit until none is left, or by arranging for both defenders to keep a controlling card in the suit. For example:

J 8 7 2

A K 5 4   Q 10 9 3

6

This is a plain suit at a slam contract and West begins with the ace (or king). Observing his partner's 10, West continues with a low card, so that both defenders retain a card higher than dummy's jack.

When discarding in a squeeze situation, a defender should follow these principles:

1. When threatened by two possible double menaces, he should discard the suit held on the left and keep a guard in the suit held on the right.

2. When there is a two-card menace which both defenders can guard, and a single menace which both can guard, the two-card menace should be kept by the defender on the left of it, the other defender keeping control of the single menace. (This accords with the general principle that menaces are less effective against the opponent who sits over them.)

3. When defending against a progressive squeeze, where the declarer is sure to gain one extra trick and threatens to gain two, discard the suit in which dummy, on your left, holds a one-card menace. This way, you have a better chance to defeat an imperfect squeeze.

DESCHAPELLES COUP

This is a defensive play named after a champion of whist. It consists of the sacrifice of a high card to establish an entry to partner's hand:

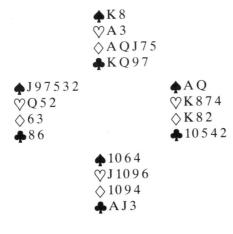

South is in 3 NT and West leads ♠5, East winning the first two tricks with the A Q.

Recognizing that the only hope is to find an entry to partner's hand, East switches to ♡K—the Deschapelles Coup. It makes no difference whether declarer takes the ace at once or holds up for one round: East, when he comes in with ◇K, will be able to put partner in with ♡Q.

The term 'Deschapelles Coup' is often attributed to a similar play where an unsupported high card is sacrificed to kill an entry in an opposing hand. This is more strictly a *Merrimac Coup*.

DEVIL'S COUP

This is a form of trump coup. The commonest example occurs when the defenders, with J x x in one hand and Q x in the other, are denied a trick. This is the typical ending:

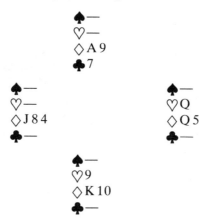

Diamonds are trumps and South leads ♡9. If West ruffs low, dummy over-ruffs with the 9 and declarer takes the balance with the two top trumps. If West ruffs with the jack, declarer over-ruffs in dummy and continues with a finesse against the queen.

This is another position where a defender's apparent trump trick is made to vanish:

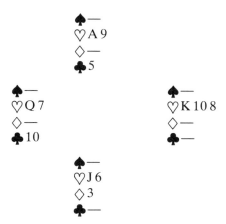

The declarer, who began with A 9 x x opposite J 6 x x in hearts, the trump suit, appears to have two certain losers, but when ♣5 is led from dummy the losers shrink to one.

DISCOVERY

A declarer who tests the lie of the cards in one suit to improve his knowledge of another is said to practise 'discovery'. This is a standard example:

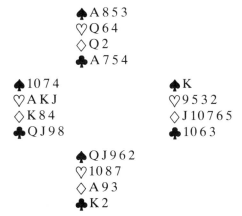

South plays in 4 ♠ after West has opened with a weak 1 NT. West leads ♡ K and switches to ♣ Q. South should win in dummy and run the queen of diamonds. When he finds that West has the king of diamonds, in addition to his other high cards, he knows enough to drop the singleton king of trumps.

For plays designed to discover the distribution, see *Counting the Hand.*

DOUBLE FINESSE

This is a finesse that will win the trick if two enemy cards are favourably placed:

(1)   A Q 10   (2)   A K 10

     x x x   x x x

In each case a finesse of the 10 is a double finesse with theoretically a slightly less than 25 per cent chance of winning the trick (slightly less than 25 per cent because, after West has followed with a low card, East has more unknown cards).

See also *Combination Finesse.*

DOUBLE SQUEEZE

A squeeze that involves both opponents is called a double squeeze. This is the purest form:

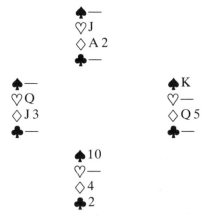

South leads ♣2 and West has to throw a diamond to keep ♡Q in front of dummy's jack. Then ♡J is discarded and East is squeezed in spades and diamonds.

For the double squeeze to operate in so economical a space, the two one-card menaces, ♡J and ♠10 in this example, must both be favourably positioned, on the left of the opponent whom they threaten.

In the above example the squeeze was simultaneous: both opponents were squeezed on the same trick. Sometimes the squeeze operates on successive tricks. It is then called non-simultaneous.

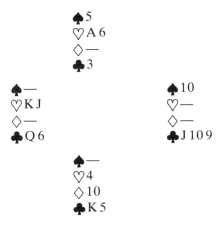

The menace cards are not so favourably placed for declarer as in the first example, but there is compensation in the presence of an extra entry in the South hand, the hand containing the squeeze card. On the lead of ◇10 West has to throw a club, so ♡6 is discarded from dummy. East is not yet under pressure, for he can spare a club, but when declarer continues with a heart to dummy's ace East is squeezed in turn.

DUCKING

A player is said to duck whenever he plays a low card instead of a higher card that might have won the trick or at least forced a high card from an opponent. This may be done for various purposes, as described in entries relating to hold-up play, avoidance play, trump control, communication play, and others.

The term refers especially to the concession of an early trick in a suit to retain communication with the opposite hand.

    (1) A Q x x x   (2) A K x x x x

          x x   x x x

In (1), supposing he has no side entry to the table and needs to develop four tricks, declarer must duck the first round of the suit and finesse the queen on the second round. In (2) the play will depend on how many tricks are needed. If six, then declarer must play for a 2–2 break; if five, he can play to the ace, then duck the second round; if four, it may be correct to duck the first round so that, if the suit turns out to be 4–0, he can duck again on the next round.

Ducking play is equally common in defence, sometimes for the same purpose of retaining a link with partner's long suit, often to prepare for a ruff (as when the lead is from a doubleton and partner holds A x x x or similar). A different and attractive form of ducking play occurs when the defender withholds a winner because he wants his partner to gain the first entry:

(3)	K 7 5		(4)	K 7 5	
J 4		A 9 3	10 4		A J 3
	Q 10 8 6 2			Q 9 8 6 2	

Assume in each case that declarer is marked with length in the suit. In (1) South leads low to the king. It is normally quite safe for East to duck when it would suit the defence for West to obtain the first entry. Similarly, in (2), if it would suit the defence for East to gain entry twice, it is safe to play low on the first round and the jack on the second round; the declarer will duck as well, hoping to bring down a doubleton ace.

DUMMY REVERSAL

A player reverses the dummy when he takes a succession of ruffs in the longer trump hand, so that in the end trumps are drawn by dummy, the shorter hand. The play occurs most often when the trump suit is divided 5–3.

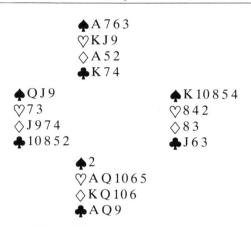

♠A 7 6 3
♡K J 9
◇A 5 2
♣K 7 4

♠Q J 9
♡7 3
◇J 9 7 4
♣10 8 5 2

♠K 10 8 5 4
♡8 4 2
◇8 3
♣J 6 3

♠2
♡A Q 10 6 5
◇K Q 10 6
♣A Q 9

South plays in 6 ♡ and West leads ♠Q. There are three possible ways of playing the hand. South could draw trumps, relying on four tricks from diamonds; he could draw two rounds of trumps, then test the diamonds (an improvement, though it fails as the cards lie); or he could play on reverse dummy lines. He begins by ruffing a spade at trick two. He can afford then to play two rounds of trumps, finishing in dummy. If trumps turn out to be 4–1 he must abandon the dummy reversal plan. Here both opponents follow to the two rounds of hearts, so South ruffs another spade, crosses to ◇A and ruffs a fourth spade with his last trump. He then leads a club to the king and draws the outstanding trump from dummy. This is the distinctive feature of reverse dummy play. Declarer has, in effect, extended his trump winners from five to six (three in dummy, three ruffs in hand).

The order in which suits are played is often critical. It is usually right to play slightly dangerous suits before the safe ones.

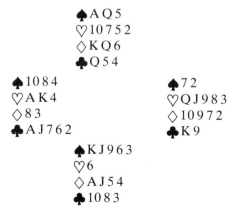

♠A Q 5
♡10 7 5 2
◇K Q 6
♣Q 5 4

♠10 8 4
♡A K 4
◇8 3
♣A J 7 6 2

♠7 2
♡Q J 9 8 3
◇10 9 7 2
♣K 9

♠K J 9 6 3
♡6
◇A J 5 4
♣10 8 3

South is in 4 ♠. West leads ♡K and, failing to find the difficult switch to a low club, plays a second heart, which South ruffs. Declarer can make ten tricks only by way of a dummy reversal, but this time it would be a mistake to begin with ♠K and a spade to the queen. The result would be that when the fourth heart was ruffed West would discard a diamond and South would be unable to enter dummy to draw the last trump. The right sequence, after the ruff at trick two, is diamond to the king, heart ruff, diamond to the queen, heart ruff with ♠J, then king of spades, draw trumps, and make the last two diamonds.

ECHELON PLAY

The term describes the familiar situation where declarer can give himself chances in different suits, so long as he tests them in the right order. A simple example occurs when declarer seeks to establish a winner by ruffing out a suit before risking a dangerous finesse. The best order of play on the two deals that follow is not so obvious.

West	*East*
♠A Q 4	♠K 7 2
♡Q 8 3	♡J 4
◇K J 9 4	◇A 6 2
♣1 0 9 7	♣A Q J 6 2

West is in 3 NT and North leads a heart to his partner's ace. South returns ♡9 and dummy's jack is allowed to win the trick. It is clear to West that he cannot afford to lose the lead. It may seem natural to place his faith in the club finesse, but it costs nothing to lay down the king and ace of diamonds first. If North has Q x, four diamond tricks can be made, enough for the contract. (If North is clever enough to drop the queen from Q 10 x, give him credit!)

West	*East*
♠Q 6	♠A 3
♡A 1 0 4 2	♡J 7
◇A 9 7 3	◇K Q 1 0 6 4
♣J 8 3	♣K 9 6 2

Again West is in 3 NT and a spade lead runs to the queen. Declarer has eight tricks in sight and may think that his best play for a ninth is to lead towards the king of clubs at an early stage.

However, he can give himself a slight extra chance by first laying down the ace of hearts. If an honour falls, a second trick can surely be established in the suit. Nothing is lost if the play of the ace of hearts proves unavailing.

ECHO (OR PETER)

A player echoes (or, in Britain, 'peters') by playing high-low. This may be done either as encouragement (see *Attitude Signals*) or to indicate an even number of cards.

In suit contracts it is normal to echo with J x but not with Q x. The play of the queen under partner's lead of the king denotes a holding of the Q J and invites partner to underlead the ace.

A dilemma may seem to arise when the partner of the opening leader holds a doubleton and knows that a second round will be ruffed, as here:

Q 9 6 3 2

A K J 5 4   10 7

8

West leads the king and East knows from the bidding that this may well be from a five-card suit. East should nevertheless 'give the count' by dropping the 10. In the present instance partner will have to guess whether or not a second round will stand up. The advantage appears when East's card is the lowest in view: the leader will then know that this card is a singleton.

It is especially important to give clear signals when declarer leads towards a long suit in a dummy.

K Q 10 9 6 3

8 7 5 2   A 4

J

Declarer leads the jack and overtakes with dummy's queen. Whether the contract is in a suit or notrumps, West must not fail to play high, so that East will know he can take the ace on the first round.

ELIMINATION

To use a boxing metaphor, it is much better in bridge to be a counter-puncher than to 'lead'. If an opponent can be persuaded to open up a suit, declarer's prospects of making tricks in the suit are never worse, and are very often much better, than if he has to lead the suit himself. The term 'elimination' refers to the process of eliminating suits that a defender could safely play, so that he will be forced later to make a disadvantageous lead.

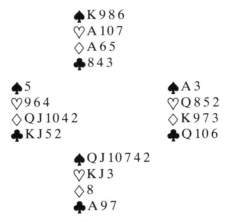

♠K986
♥A107
♦A65
♣843

♠5
♥964
♦QJ1042
♣KJ52

♠A3
♥Q852
♦K973
♣Q106

♠QJ107 42
♥KJ3
♦8
♣A97

South is in 4 ♠ and West leads ♦Q. It is evident that declarer, with two losers in clubs and one in trumps, needs to avoid a heart loser. He can avoid the need to finesse by this sequence: ace of diamonds, ruff a diamond, force out ace of spades; draw the remaining trump, ruff a third diamond, play ace of clubs and exit with a club. At this stage the defenders must either lead a heart or concede a ruff-and-discard, enabling South to dispose of his heart loser. If declarer had failed to eliminate diamonds by ruffing the second and third rounds, the end-play would not have been effective.

Sometimes the declarer has to rely on a partial or imperfect elimination, depending for its success on a favourable lie of the cards.

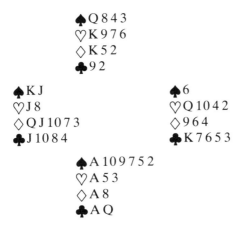

♠Q843
♡K976
◇K52
♣92

♠KJ
♡J8
◇QJ1073
♣J1084

♠6
♡Q1042
◇964
♣K7653

♠A109752
♡A53
◇A8
♣AQ

South is in 6 ♠ and a diamond is led. The first hope fails when the king of spades does not fall under the ace. South appears now to have a loser in hearts and a loser in trumps, but he still has fair chances. He must risk the club finesse, cash ♣A, and eliminate diamonds by ruffing the third round. Then he cashes ace and king of hearts before exiting with a trump. He is in luck, because the hand with ♠K has no more hearts and must concede a ruff-and-discard.

END PLAY

This name may be given to any special stroke that takes place in the end game, usually a squeeze, throw-in or trump coup. Most players, however, reserve the use of the term for a forced lead: a player is the victim of an end play when any lead he makes will cost a trick. See *Elimination* and *Throw-in*.

ENTRY-KILLING PLAY

There are several plays by second hand which have the effect of killing or disrupting the declarer's entries to a long suit in the opposite hand. These plays are important when there are no other entries.

AJ105

K73   Q84

962

South leads the 2, intending to play the 10 from dummy. By going up with the king, West holds declarer to two tricks.

AJ963

Q105   K84

72

On the lead of the 2 West must go up with the queen. Otherwise, declarer will put in the 9 and East will either have to let this win or give South the chance to make four tricks by finessing the jack on the next round.

The same kind of play is available to declarer at the expense of defenders:

Q105

72   AJ963

K84

Suppose that West leads the 7 against a notrump contract. If he can read the position, declarer can break the run of the suit by going in with dummy's queen.

For other plays concerned with entry, see *Avoidance Play, Blocking Play, Deschapelles Coup, Ducking, Hold-up Play, Merrimac Coup, Scissors Coup* and *Unblocking Play*.

FALSE-CARDING

When a defender departs from convention to mislead the declarer he is said to false-card. This is a simple example:

AJ103

874   KQ

9652

South leads low and finesses the jack. The conventional card for East is the queen, the lower of cards in sequence. The play of the king would be a false card, though not, in this familiar situation, one to which the declarer would pay much attention.

There are numerous positions where the play by a defender of a higher card than necessary may cause declarer to misguess on the next round. These are some examples:

(1)	Q 10 8 6 5		(2)	Q 10 3	
J 7 2		K 9 4	A J 9		7 5 2
	A 3			K 8 6 4	

In (1) South leads the ace. If East drops the 4 South will probably finesse the 10 on the next round. If East false-cards with the 9, declarer will probably go up with the queen next time, playing East for J 9 alone. (If East has K 9, to finesse the 10 will not gain.) In (2) South leads low from hand. West's jack is a dead card in the sense that declarer doubtless intends to finesse the 10. But suppose West inserts the jack: declarer may return the 10 to the ace and subsequently finesse the 8.

(3)	Q 7 4		(4)	J 9 5	
10 9 5		K 3	8 6 4		Q 10
	A J 8 6 2			A K 7 3 2	

These are examples of 'obligatory' false cards. When in (3) South leads low to the jack West must drop the 9 (or 10). Declarer may later lead the queen from dummy, hoping to pin a doubleton 10 9. In (4) South leads the ace (or king). If East drops the queen he may induce the declarer to finesse the 9 on the next round, playing West for 10 x x x.

FINESSE

A finesse is an attempt to profit from a favourable lie of the adverse cards. Taking advantage of the positional factor, a player tries to win or establish a trick with a card that one of his opponents could beat. The following are examples of the simple finesse:

(1)	A Q	(2)	A x x
	x x		Q J 10

In (1) South leads low and plays the queen from dummy, hoping the king lies with west. In (2) South leads the queen from hand.

There are many situations where a direct finesse is playable but is not the best way to obtain the maximum number of tricks.

(3) A Q x x   (4) Q J x x

J x   A x x

In (3) the best play to develop three tricks is to lead low from dummy towards the jack, intending to duck the next round if the jack holds. The plan succeeds if East has the king, no more than twice guarded. In (4), to make as many tricks as possible, South leads twice towards the Q J.

See also *Backward Finesse, Combination Finesse, Double Finesse, Finesse Against Dummy, Finesse Against Partner, Ruffing Finesse* and *Two-way Finesse.*

FINESSE AGAINST DUMMY

A player is said to finesse against dummy when, on partner's lead, he plays a middle card from his hand, retaining a higher card over an honour in dummy. This is a common situation:

Q 8 3

J 9 5 4   K 10 6

A 7 2

When West leads the 4 and dummy plays low, East must insert the 10, retaining the king to capture dummy's queen.

Another common example:

A 10 4

K 9 5 3   J 8 2

Q 7 6

West leads the 3 and dummy plays low. If East plays the jack he allows declarer to take three tricks. East must play the 8, a finesse against dummy's 10.

FINESSE AGAINST PARTNER

There is an important difference between a finesse against dummy and a finesse against partner. This last manoeuvre has gained its bad reputation from positions of this kind:

5

Q 10 8 6 3   K 9 4

A J 7 2

West leads the 6. If East, fearful of surrender to declarer's possible A Q J, withholds the king, he costs his side a trick.

There are nevertheless occasions when a finesse against partner (which means simply the refusal to play third hand high when dummy holds no honour card) is eminently correct.

6 4

J 9 7 5 2   A Q 3

K 10 8

West leads the 5 against 3 NT. Especially if East holds a fairly strong hand (suggesting that partner may not hold a quick entry), he should play the queen, to induce declarer to part with the king.

9 4 2

Q 7 6 5 3   K J 8

A 10

West leads the 5 against a suit contract. East should play the jack rather than the king, mainly because this play will establish who holds the queen. If East's king loses to the ace he will not know whether there is another trick to be made in the suit.

FORCING TACTICS (IN PLAY)

The defenders are said to play a forcing game when they set out to weaken declarer's trump holding by forcing him to ruff a side suit. Such tactics are often adopted when a defender has length in trumps and hopes to gain trump control.

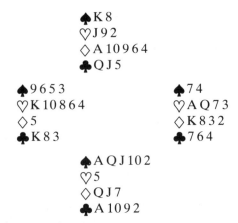

A forcing lead, a heart, is the only one to break four spades. After ruffing a heart and drawing trumps, declarer loses control when he takes a losing finesse in a minor suit.

On a club or spade lead, the hand is straightforward. On a diamond, declarer must play with care. He must go up with the ace and unblock with the queen or jack from hand. Then he draws trumps and leads his remaining diamond honour. If East wins, declarer takes four tricks in diamonds and six in the black suits; if East ducks, declarer switches to clubs.

GRAND COUP

This is simply a trump coup with the distinguishing feature that, when declarer is reducing his trump length to prepare for the characteristic ending, the cards that he ruffs are winners. The name dates from the days of whist, when such a play was thought deserving of a special name.

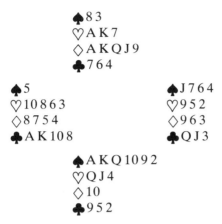

Against 4 ♠ the defenders cash three club tricks and switch to a diamond, which South wins in hand.

South plays the A K of trumps and when West shows out he has to execute a trump coup. In this instance the coup involves ruffing two diamonds, to arrive at this ending, with the lead in dummy:

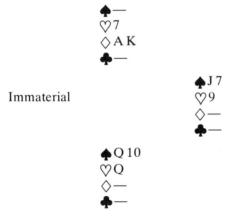

Dummy leads a diamond and East, whether he ruffs now or later, makes notrump trick. The fact that declarer had to ruff winners to bring about this ending makes it a grand coup; in fact, a double grand coup, since two winners were ruffed. It is possible to construct a quadruple and even a quintuple grand coup.

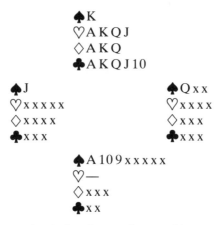

Against any lead, South can shorten his trumps five times and pick up East's queen, to make seven spades.

See also *Trump Coup*.

GROSVENOR COUP

The Grosvenor coup (or Grosvenor gambit) is a jocose name for a type of play that presents an opponent with a chance of which he cannot logically avail himself. Suppose that a suit is distributed in this way:

K 9 6 4

Q J 3   10

A 8 7 5 2

On South's lead of the ace West drops the jack (or queen). South has a chance now to pick up the suit without loss, but he can scarcely imagine that West has given him this opportunity.

A play that gives the declarer a chance to win an 'impossible' trick may on occasions be made for deceptive or tactical reasons; but when it is done from whimsy or non-comprehension, it is a Grosvenor.

GUARD SQUEEZE

This is a squeeze in which one defender has to protect the other from a possible finesse.

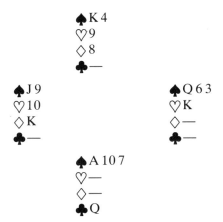

♠ K 4
♡ 9
◇ 8
♣ —

♠ J 9   ♠ Q 6 3
♡ 10   ♡ K
◇ K   ◇ —
♣ —   ♣ —

♠ A 10 7
♡ —
◇ —
♣ Q

South leads ♣Q and among the pressures to which West is subjected is the need to protect his partner from a finesse in spades. For the moment West can let go ♡10. Then dummy throws ◇8 and East is squeezed in spades and hearts.

It will be noted that the 9 of hearts is a one-card threat controlled by both opponents, yet it is an essential part of the squeeze. This is a characteristic of the guard squeeze. Except in a few complicated positions (the rare 'clash squeeze') a one-card threat which both opponents control is of no value against best defence.

HOLD-UP PLAY

A player is said to hold up when for tactical reasons he declines to play a winning card. Usually his object is to break communication between the enemy hands, but there may be other reasons too.

Here is a simple hold-up to break communication:

x x

K Q J x x   x x x

A x x

At a notrump contract declarer holds up the ace until the third round. If East gains the lead he will have no card of the suit to return.

A declarer who has a double guard may still hold up:

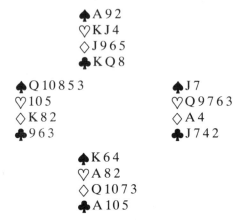

```
              ♠A92
              ♡KJ4
              ◇J965
              ♣KQ8
♠Q10853                    ♠J7
♡105                       ♡Q9763
◇K82                       ◇A4
♣963                       ♣J742
              ♠K64
              ♡A82
              ◇Q1073
              ♣A105
```

West leads ♠5 against 3 NT, dummy plays low and East plays the jack. If declarer wins with the king and tries to establish diamonds, East will win and the second spade guard will be removed while West still has ◇K.

By holding up the spade at trick one, declarer ensures the contract unless a defender with five spades holds both ace and king of diamonds.

Hold-ups are equally common in defence. In the next example declarer is trying to establish this suit at a notrump contract. Dummy has a side entry, which the defenders cannot force out.

```
              QJ109xx
     Ax                    Kxx
              xx
```

When South leads low to the queen, both defenders must hold up; then the suit can never be brought in.

In many cases Hold-up and Ducking are alternative names for the same manoeuvre. Under *Ducking* an example is given of a duck by a defender who wants to give partner a ruff. This is the other side of the coin:

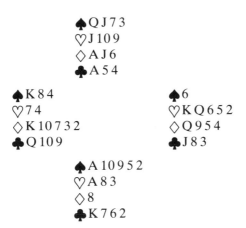

Against South's contract of 4 ♠ West leads ♡ 7 and East plays the queen. If declarer takes the trick West will come in with the king of trumps and get a heart ruff. But if declarer plays West for a doubleton and holds up the ace, he breaks the communications.

Alter the heart position a little and the hold-up may still be necessary:

J 10 x

x x x   K Q 9 x

A x x

West leads a heart, dummy plays the 10 and East the queen. Reading East for K Q, South holds up the ace. Then East cannot continue without conceding a trick.

Hold-up for other tactical reasons

As was mentioned earlier, there are also hold-ups that are not primarily concerned with communication. This is an example:

K Q 10 x

J x x   A 9 x

x x x

South leads small to dummy's king and East holds up. Later, when South leads a second round, he does not know whether to put on the queen or the 10.

Clearly, if East releases the ace on the first round South is likely to take a winning finesse of the 10 on the second round. Many more plays are based on the same idea.

There are some important hold-up plays which involve the trump suit. (See also *Trump Control*.) This is an example:

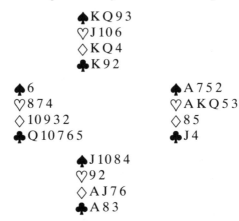

```
                ♠KQ93
                ♡J106
                ◇KQ4
                ♣K92
  ♠6                          ♠A752
  ♡874                        ♡AKQ53
  ◇10932                      ◇85
  ♣Q10765                     ♣J4
                ♠J1084
                ♡92
                ◇AJ76
                ♣A83
```

South is in 4♠ and the defenders begin with three rounds of hearts. South ruffs the third heart and leads trumps.

Now East must hold up his ace for two rounds. If declarer were to play a third round East would win and play hearts, forcing the last trump from dummy and setting the contract two tricks. Declarer's best plan therefore is to cut his losses and abandon trumps, permitting East to make his small trump for a one-trick set.

INTRA-FINESSE

This play was named by the Brazilian expert, Gabriel Chagas. Declarer takes a losing finesse on the first round so that he can play to pin an honour on the next.

```
               Q853
  J7                          K104
               A962
```

Declarer can hold the defenders to one trick by playing small towards the dummy and finessing the 8. East wins with the 10 and a later lead of the queen pins the jack.

JOURNALIST LEADS

The system of leads so described became well known after an article in an American magazine, but most of the ideas were developed in Scandinavia.

Honour leads against notrumps

Ace: asks partner to unblock with K, Q or J, or to give count by issuing a normal suit-length signal. (But against 3 NT, when the bidding suggests that this contract is based on a long suit, the lead of an ace requests 'attitude'.)

King: From A K or K Q.

Queen: Q J, A Q J, possibly K Q 10 (with either the nine or appreciable length) or A Q 10.

Jack: J 10, no higher honour.

Ten: A J 10, K J 10, A 10 9, K 10 9, Q 10 9. The 10 is therefore a 'strong lead'.

Nine: 10 9, no higher honour.

Spot-card leads against notrumps

The object here is to show the leader's 'attitude' in respect of the suit he has chosen. If he wants his suit to be returned he leads his lowest; if not, he leads the highest spot card he can afford. Thus from A Q 7 5 3 2 the lead is the 2, from 6 5 3 2 the 6.

Honour leads against suit contracts

From two or more touching honours the second highest is led. A lead of the ace denies the king, the king shows A K, and so on.

Spot-card leads against suit contracts

Third best is led from an even number, lowest from an odd number.

LAVINTHAL DISCARDS

It is possible to attach suit-preference meaning to discards. A high discard asks for the higher-ranking of the two remaining suits, a low discard for the lower-ranking.

♠K 8 6
♡A Q 9 3
◇7 2
♣Q J 10 4

♠A Q J 3
♡J 8 6 5
◇J 8 5
♣7 3

South is in 3 NT and West leads ◇ 4 to the jack and king. Declarer plays on clubs and West wins the third round with the ace. It might be a mistake for East to let go a heart, and he does not want to part with a spade, if only because partner might hold 10 x x. To signify that he wants a spade switch, he discards the 8 of diamonds.

LEADS AGAINST NOTRUMPS

The traditional lead from various suit combinations is as follows:

From three honours in sequence, the top card, except that the king is led from A K Q.

From a broken sequence, such as K Q 10 or Q J 9, the top card (but king from A K J).

From an interior sequence, such as K J 10 or Q 10 9, the higher of the touching honours.

From other long suits, fourth best, the 6 from A K 8 6 3.

From a suit bid by partner, or from a short unbid suit, the higher of touching honours, the top card from a doubleton or three small.

The lead of an ace against notrumps has two possible meanings: it may signify a short suit, A K x, or it may be from a long suit such as A K J x x x, in which case it is a request to partner to drop an honour or to indicate three cards by playing the highest.

Opening leads are the subject of much innovation and it may well be that even the long-established lead of the fourth best itself is on the way out. See *Buso, Journalist Leads*, and *MUD*.

LEADS AGAINST TRUMP CONTRACT

The main difference from the lead against notrumps is that the higher of touching honours is led, the queen from Q J x x, not the fourth best, and it is normal to lead, rather than underlead, an ace. The traditional lead from a suit headed by A K is the king, with the ace signifying a doubleton A K. However, it is now equally common to follow the opposite method, leading the ace from A K x, the king from A K alone.

For specialized leads, see *Ace from A-K, Buso, Journalist Leads, MUD, Rusinow Leads.*

LOSER-ON-LOSER PLAY

To lead (or play) a losing card from one hand and discard a loser from another suit is a tactical move with many variations. A common reason for the play is to prevent trump promotion by the defence.

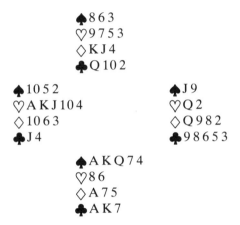

```
                    ♠863
                    ♡9753
                    ◇KJ4
                    ♣Q102
    ♠1052                        ♠J9
    ♡AKJ104                      ♡Q2
    ◇1063                        ◇Q982
    ♣J4                          ♣98653
                    ♠AKQ74
                    ♡86
                    ◇A75
                    ♣AK7
```

South is in 4 ♠ and the defence begins with ♡ K A J. If East ruffs the third heart South must not over-ruff. If he does, he will lose a trump trick and later a diamond. Instead, South must throw his losing diamond.

Loser-on-loser to avoid an over-ruff

When there is a loser to ruff in dummy, but reason to believe that the next defender will over-ruff, a solution may be to discard a loser in another suit, preparing later to ruff that suit.

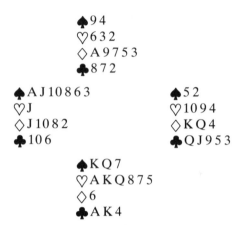

South plays in 4 ♡ after West has overcalled in spades. West leads ◇ J, taken by dummy's ace. A spade to the king falls to the ace, and West switches to a trump.

Declarer needs a ruff in dummy for an overtrick. All the indications are that East will be able to over-ruff the third round of spades. South therefore discards a losing club from dummy on the third spade. As the cards lie, he will make his extra trick by ruffing the third round of clubs.

Loser-on-loser elimination

Declarer often prepares for an elimination ending by discarding a loser on a loser.

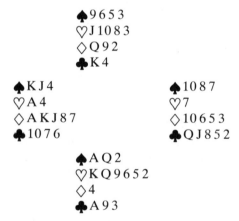

West opens 1 ◇ but the final contract is 4 ♡ by South. West leads ◇ K and switches to ace and another trump.

Expecting the spade finesse to be wrong, declarer plans an elimination combined with loser-on-loser play. He ruffs dummy's ◇9, plays ♣K A and enters dummy with a third-round club ruff. Then he leads ◇Q and discards ♠2, leaving West on play.

Loser-on-loser play occurs in some forms of avoidance (see *Scissors Coup*) and squeeze play (see *Rectifying the Count*).

McKENNEY CONVENTION

See *Suit Preference Signal*.

MENACE

This is an alternative name for threat—a card that threatens an opponent's holding in a squeeze position.

MERRIMAC COUP

This is the sacrificial lead of an unsupported high card with the object of knocking out a vital entry in declarer's hand or dummy. (Compare the *Deschapelles Coup*, which is similar but less common.) The usual occasion for the Merrimac Coup is when dummy has a long suit and only one outside entry.

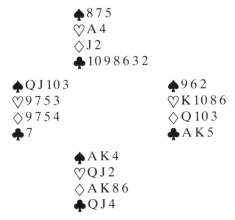

```
                    ♠875
                    ♡A4
                    ◇J2
                    ♣1098632
    ♠QJ103                      ♠962
    ♡9753                       ♡K1086
    ◇9754                       ◇Q103
    ♣7                          ♣AK5
                    ♠AK4
                    ♡QJ2
                    ◇AK86
                    ♣QJ4
```

West leads ♠Q against 3 NT. South wins and attacks clubs. East ducks the first round of clubs and wins the second, West discarding a heart.

It is clear that dummy's entry, ♡A, must be removed before the clubs are established. East, therefore, leads ♡K, the Merrimac Coup. This gives away a sure heart trick but prevents dummy's long suit from being brought in. Careful defence now beats the contract.

MORTON'S FORK

The term describes the situation (see *Waiting Move*) when declarer leads low from (say) Q x to dummy's K x x and the defender who holds the ace under dummy is in a dilemma: if he plays the ace he presents the declarer with two tricks in the suit, and if he ducks he may allow the queen to be discarded on a winner in another suit.

The name is derived from Cardinal Morton, Chancellor under King Henry VII, who employed a system that would commend itself to modern tax-gatherers. If a merchant lived well, then clearly he could afford to contribute to the Royal Treasury, and if he lived frugally it was equally clear that he had money to spare.

MUD LEADS (MIDDLE, UP, DOWN)

In this convention the opening lead from three small is the middle card, followed on the next round by the highest card. For example, the 6 from 7 6 4 is followed by the 7, and partner then knows that a third card is held. When the lead is top-of-nothing, the 7 followed by the 6 does not indicate whether the lead is from two cards or three.

MUD is not used in a suit bid by partner. If the leader has supported the suit, he leads his highest to deny an honour; if he has not supported the suit, he leads the lowest to give an immediate count.

ODD-EVEN SIGNALS

See *Roman (Odd-Even) Signals.*

OPENING LEAD

See *Leads Against Notrumps* and *Leads Against Trump Contract,* and the references mentioned there.

OPTIMUM STRATEGY

There are many situations in defence where a certain line of play is considered most likely to cause declarer to go wrong, but if this line of play is consistently followed its effect is diminished. This is a familiar example:

(1)   A J 9 x   (2)   A J 9 x

    K 10 x   Q x x   K Q x   10 x x

              x x x   x x x

In (1) South leads low from hand. If West plays low, the best chance for three tricks is, superficially, to insert the 9, gaining against Q 10 x and K 10 x, losing only against K Q x. For this reason it is normal for an experienced defender to play the king (assuming that he places his partner with the queen). Declarer will then have a more open guess on the second round.

But now look at the other situation, shown in (2). When West plays low, expecting South to follow percentages and finesse the 9, South may say to himself, 'If West had held K 10 x or Q 10 x he would have played a high honour. His low card suggests K Q x, so I will play the jack from dummy.' Thus the declarer, against an opponent who consistently follows the 'correct' play (as opposed to an optimum strategy) will seldom go wrong.

Much thought has been given to another position where similar considerations arise:

(3)   A 9 x   (4)   A 9 x

    J x x   Q x x   Q J   x x x

              K 10 x   K 10 x

If East, in the end game, has to open up this suit, the standard play in (3) is the queen. South, being aware of this, should normally play for split honours, because East is mathematically more likely to hold three to an honour than Q J x. (With Q J x he might have led the queen *or* the jack: see *Restricted Choice*.) Furthermore, when in (4) East leads a low card, South may judge that East holds neither honour and may bring down West's doubleton Q J.

It is possible in situations of this sort to work out an optimum strategy for the defender, who denies his opponent these inferences by varying his play according to exact proportions. Such exercises have little practical meaning, as the strategy is valid only if one plays endlessly against the same opponent. But the conclusion is important: a defender must vary his play and not be easy to read.

OVERTAKING SQUEEZE

This is a rare position in which there must be trumps in both hands when the squeeze begins.

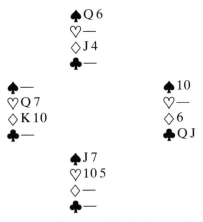

Playing in spades, South cannot crossruff the last four tricks because East will over-ruff the dummy. South therefore leads the jack of spades and, depending on which suit West unguards, overtakes or not with dummy's queen of spades.

PETER

See *Echo*.

PROBABILITIES OF DISTRIBUTION

In the absence of any other information, a declarer can judge the likely distribution of the defender's cards in a suit by reference to mathematical probabilities. At the start of the hand the probabilities, assuming the bidding has thrown no light, are as follows:

When the defenders have between them	These are likely to be divided	Percentage probability
seven cards	4–3	62
	5–2	31
	6–1	7
six cards	4–2	48
	3–3	36
	5–1	15
five cards	3–2	68
	4–1	28
	5–0	4
four cards	3–1	50
	2–2	40
	4–0	10
three cards	2–1	78
	3–0	22
two cards	1–1	52
	2–0	48

It will be seen that when defenders have an odd number of cards in a suit a favourable break (4–3, 3–2, 2–1) is odds-on. But when the defenders have an even number of cards, the even distributions 3–3 and 2–2 are odds-against.

These expectancies change constantly as the play progresses. After both defenders have followed suit to early rounds, the more even divisions become more likely. Consider this combination:

A J 7 4 2

K 6

The chance of a 3–3 break is initially 36 per cent, but if the A K are played off and the queen does not appear, the chance is now 52 per cent. This is because the 5–1 and 6–0 distributions have been eliminated, and also the 4–2 distributions where the queen is doubleton. The only *a priori* possibilities remaining are Q x x x opposite x x and Q x x opposite x x x, the second of these being mathematically more likely.

The mathematical probabilities within a given suit may also change without the suit being played. Suppose the declarer starts out with four hearts opposite three and that after ten tricks neither defender has played a heart. Then they *must* be divided 3–3. The further the play has advanced, the more likely is an even break.

PROGRESSIVE SQUEEZE

This is a squeeze that wins two extra tricks against an opponent who is threatened in three suits. There is usually an extended menace in the hand opposite the squeeze card.

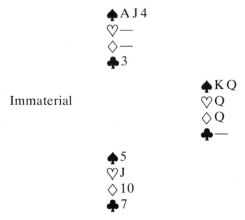

Playing at notrumps, South leads ♣7. East cannot let go a spade without giving dummy the remaining tricks. Whether East discards a diamond or a heart, he is squeezed again when the suit he has unguarded is led on the next trick.

When there is no extended menace, as in the spade suit above, there must be two 2-card threats in different hands and there must also be a one-card threat on the left of the opponent to be squeezed. The minimum compass is five cards.

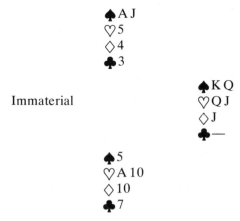

When ♣7 is led, East is squeezed in three suits. Whichever suit he lets go, he will be squeezed again a trick or two later. Although he has only three clear winners, South makes all five tricks.

PSEUDO-SQUEEZE

A pseudo-squeeze occurs when a defender, not genuinely squeezed, throws the wrong card. Certain techniques are available to pose a problem for the defenders. Two such techniques are described below.

Most players, when they hope for a pseudo-squeeze, tend to begin by cashing the suits in which they have no potential menace. This is not necessarily best.

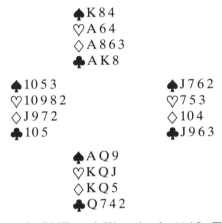

```
              ♠K 8 4
              ♡A 6 4
              ◇A 8 6 3
              ♣A K 8
♠10 5 3                      ♠J 7 6 2
♡10 9 8 2                    ♡7 5 3
◇J 9 7 2                     ◇10 4
♣10 5                        ♣J 9 6 3
              ♠A Q 9
              ♡K Q J
              ◇K Q 5
              ♣Q 7 4 2
```

The contract is 7 NT and West leads ♡10. There are three winners in each suit, and a 3–3 break in clubs or diamonds will give South the contract. There will also be an automatic squeeze if either opponent has four clubs and four diamonds. South wants to find the best sequence of play to provide the additional chance of a defensive error.

Most players, hoping for a club or diamond discard, would begin by cashing the major suits. It is better, however, to begin with three rounds of diamonds. Nothing is lost by this as neither defender, seeing the four-card length in dummy, will discard a diamond if the other suits are led first.

The advantage occurs when one defender has clubs and length in one of the major suits, as East has here. On the third diamond East can discard a heart, but South now takes three rounds of hearts, forcing East to discard again. This time he has a problem and may part with a club. By playing in this way South does not forgo the chance of a genuine squeeze.

If South begins by cashing three tricks in each major suit East has no problem, as he can see that ♠J is redundant.

The principle is that, if it can be done without spoiling the entries for a legitimate squeeze, declarer should cash first the winners in the suit where the length is visible in dummy.

Another way of confusing the opposition is to leave a control on the table that is only an apparent threat, because the declarer in fact cannot reach it. Meanwhile, he holds a hidden threat in his own hand.

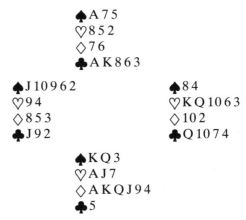

South plays 7 ◊ and a spade is led. Declarer lacks entries to profit from a 4–3 break in clubs and the chances of a genuine squeeze are very slim indeed. His best play is to cash just one top club in dummy, then run off winners, arriving at this position:

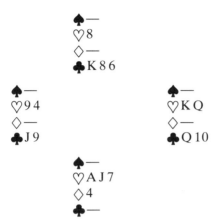

When the last trump is led, East, thinking that South has a second club, may be deceived into throwing a heart, playing his partner for a guard in this suit. Similar confusion might arise if the heart honours were divided, both players clinging to a guard in clubs. Such accidents can be prevented by defenders who are pernickety in their discarding, but life is not always like that.

RECTIFYING THE COUNT

Many squeezes can be executed only when the declarer is able to win all the remaining tricks but one. Any manoeuvre that aims at bringing about this situation is known as 'rectifying the count'.

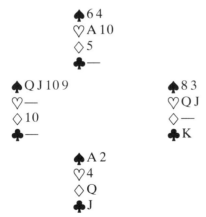

Playing at notrumps, South needs four of the last five tricks. West is on lead and plays ♠Q.

Declarer has only three natural tricks but the elements of an automatic squeeze against East are present. Dummy's hearts are a two-card menace, ♣J is a single menace, and ◇Q is a potential squeeze card.

However, the timing is not right, inasmuch as South cannot win all the remaining tricks but one. If he wins the spade lead and cashes ◇Q East will be able to throw a spade and the squeeze will not operate. Instead, South ducks the lead of ♠Q. He wins the next trick, either a spade or a diamond, and plays off his other winner to squeeze East.

This stratagem of ducking an early trick (also called a 'submarine squeeze') is very common. Whenever there is a prospect of a squeeze, declarer counts the number of cards remaining and tries to bring about the situation in which he can win with top cards all the tricks but one. In this example declarer rectifies the count with the aid of loser-on-loser-play:

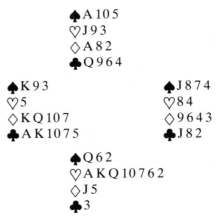

♠A 10 5
♡J 9 3
◇A 8 2
♣Q 9 6 4

♠K 9 3   ♠J 8 7 4
♡5   ♡8 4
◇K Q 10 7   ◇9 6 4 3
♣A K 10 7 5   ♣J 8 2

♠Q 6 2
♡A K Q 10 7 6 2
◇J 5
♣3

South plays in 4 ♡ after West has opened 1 ♣. West leads ♣K and switches to ◇K, which is allowed to hold. East shows an even number by his play of the 6, so West continues with ◇Q, forcing dummy's ace.

Declarer can foresee a three-card ending in which West, holding ♠K x and ♣A, will be squeezed in front of dummy's ♠A 10 and ♣Q. However, the timing is not right, because South has lost only two tricks so far. To rectify the count, he draws trumps and plays a third diamond, discarding a spade from hand. Neither defender can safely attack spades and the squeeze is effective.

RESTRICTED CHOICE

The Principle of Restricted Choice is expressed by Terence Reese in *The Expert Game* as follows: 'A defender should be assumed not to have had a choice rather than to have exercised a choice in a particular way.' By following this idea, a declarer can adopt the best mathematical chance in many suit combinations where he has a choice. For example:

(1) A 10 8 6 4   (2) A 9 7 3

K 7 5 3   K Q 2

In (1) South plays the king and East follows with the queen or jack. On the next round does South finesse or play for the drop? In (2) declarer plays off the K Q and East drops an honour, the jack or the 10, on the second round. When South leads low to the third round and West follows, South has to decide whether to finesse the 9.

In each case declarer should assume that East's choice was restricted. In (1) he assumes that East played the honour because it was a singleton, rather than that East exercised a choice with Q J bare. In (2), if East has played the 10 on the second round, declarer assumes that he began with 10 x, for again with J 10 x East would have had a choice.

It will be found that the Principle of Restricted Choice conforms to *a priori* expectations. In (1) the two holdings, singleton queen and singleton jack, together are more likely than the one holding, Q J bare. In (2) the two combinations, J x and 10 x, are mathematically more likely than the combination J 10 x.

The same principle can be extended to situations where a defender has a choice not between two cards but between two suits. Against 6 NT, no suit having been mentioned, West leads from a holding of what turns out to be three small cards. Later, declarer has to decide whether in another suit West holds three small cards or Q x x. The fact that West chose to lead the first suit affords a presumption that his choice was restricted and that he had not the same holding in both suits. It is therefore logical to place West with the queen of the other suit. The argument is: with ♣ x x x and ♢ x x x he might have led, say, a diamond instead of a club. Since he chose a club, perhaps his diamonds are Q x x.

REVERSE DUMMY PLAY

See *Dummy Reversal.*

REVERSE SIGNALS

Since the earliest days of bridge, players have dropped a high card to encourage a lead and a low one to discourage. There are good grounds for reversing this system, both for economy and clarity.

Q 10 8 2

A 6   K J 9 3

7 5 4

When West leads the ace, East cannot afford the 9 as an encouraging card. He must play the 3 and hope that partner will understand. Playing reverse signals, the 3 from East would be encouraging.

Supporters of reverse, or 'upside down', signals point out also that when a player wishes to discourage a lead, the play of a high card is more certain to convey the message. The following is a common situation:

6 3

K Q 10 7   9 8 4

A J 5 2

West leads the king against a notrump contract. East plays the 4 and declarer will usually drop the 5 as a deceptive measure. Now East cannot be sure of the true position—his partner may be trying to encourage from the A 4 2 or J 4 2, or the 4 may be his lowest card or the beginning of a high-low signal from 9 8 4 2.

Playing reverse signals, East will drop the 9 to discourage a continuation. This will make the situation immediately clear.

ROMAN LEADS

See *Rusinow Leads.*

ROMAN (ODD-EVEN) SIGNALS

Some European players use the parity of the cards played—odd or even—to express encouragement or discouragement. To encourage his partner's lead, a defender plays an odd-numbered card; to discourage, he plays an even-numbered card.

When playing an even card to discourage, the defender with a choice of cards to play may be able to issue at the same time a suit-preference signal. Suppose that East is defending against a heart contract and West leads ♠A. Holding ♠8 5 4, East may play the 8 to ask for a diamond switch, the 4 to ask for a club.

A problem arises when the defender has no card of the required parity. Suppose partner leads the king of a suit and the defender has Q 8 2. He wants to encourage, but has no odd card. In this situation the Roman practice is to play the even card that would call for an improbable suit-preference, in the hope that partner will be able to read the situation.

When the defender wants to discourage but has no even cards, holding perhaps 7 5 3, he discards the lowest, hoping that partner will be able to judge that no even card is available.

It is also possible to use the odd-even idea to express suit-preference when discarding. Discarding from Q 8 7 3 2 for example, a defender has three choices: the 7 to request this suit, the 8 or 2 to suggest a shift to the higher or lower of the alternative suits.

RUFF-AND-DISCARD

When the declarer is able to ruff a defender's lead in one hand, while discarding a loser from the other, he is said to obtain a ruff-and-discard, often called 'a ruff and sluff'. For example:

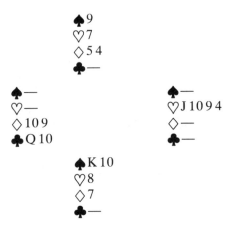

Spades are trumps and South exits with a heart. East wins and has to return the suit, giving a ruff-and-discard. Declarer naturally elects to ruff in dummy and discard the losing diamond from his own hand.

An end position of this kind, where the defender has to concede a ruff-and-discard, can often be brought about by elimination play. The diagram position resulted from the following simple elimination:

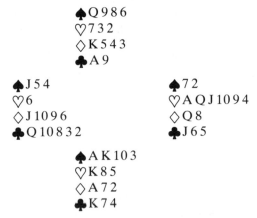

South is playing in 4 ♠ after East has overcalled in hearts. East wins the first trick with ♡ A and returns the queen, which is covered by South and ruffed by West. West leads ◇ J. South wins and draws trumps in two rounds.

Having lost two tricks, declarer still has a loser in each red suit and his only chance to dispose of one is by a ruff-and-discard. This can be achieved if East started with fewer than three diamonds. Declarer eliminates clubs, ruffing the third round in dummy, and cashes ◇ K. Then he puts East in with a heart, as shown earlier.

RUFFING FINESSE

This term describes the situation where an opponent's high card (if played) can be ruffed, establishing other cards as winners.

(1) KQJx	(2) AQJ10
Void	x

In (1) dummy leads the king of a side suit. If East plays the ace South ruffs, but if East plays low the king is allowed to run.

In (2) South may play either defender for the king but a ruffing finesse against East will usually be superior, as if West holds the king it may be too well guarded to bring down.

When discards are needed, the ruffing finesse is often a safer line of play than a straight finesse.

♠Q4
♡AQJ10
◇10853
♣AK7

♠AKJ985
♡8
◇A6
♣10962

The contract is 6 ♠ and West leads ◇ Q. South draws trumps, cashes ♡ A and leads the queen, discarding his losing diamond if East plays low. Whether the finesse succeeds or not, South is home, but if he takes the straight finesse he may lose at once a heart and a diamond.

RULE OF ELEVEN

When a player leads fourth best from a long suit the number of that card, when subtracted from 11, will tell how many higher cards are held by the other three hands.

The Rule of Eleven assists all the players to judge the lie of the cards. It helps the leader's partner in a situation such as the following:

K 10 3

6 led   A Q 8

Defending against notrumps, West leads the 6 and dummy plays low. Taking the lead to be fourth best, East applies the Rule of Eleven. He subtracts 6 from 11 and concludes that there are 5 higher cards than the 6 not in the leader's hand. Since all 5 are visible to him, he can judge that South has no high card. East can play the 8 in the assurance that it will hold the trick.

Declarer can draw a useful conclusion in a situation of this kind:

K 8 4

A 10 6 2

West leads the 5, dummy plays low, and East's jack is taken by the ace. The rule tells South that East has no other card better than the 5. To make three tricks, therefore, he does not try to drop the queen or 9 in East's hand. He leads towards dummy and finesses the 8 if West does not split his Q 9.

The explanation of the rule is simple. Imagine that the cards are numbered from 2 (the deuce) up to 14 (the ace). By subtracting the number of the card led from 14 we obtain the total number of higher cards in all four hands. Three of those cards are known to be held by the opening leader, so to discover the number held by the other three players we subtract from 11.

In the same way, if a defender, following a different convention, has led fifth best, the number of the card led should be subtracted from 10.

RUSINOW LEADS

Rusinow leads apply to the lead of an unbid suit against a trump contract. The principle is to lead the second-ranking of touching honours. Thus the king is led from A K x, the queen from K Q J x, and so on. When an ace is led, the king is known to be missing.

The procedure is reversed with two bare honours. When a player leads the king and continues with the queen, partner knows that he has no more.

Roman Leads employ the same principle and extend it to no-trump contracts. Against notrumps, an additional rule applies: the 10 is always from an interior sequence such as Q 10 9, K 10 9 or K J 10. From J 10 9, the lead is the jack, not the 10.

SAFETY PLAY

This term applies most accurately to situations where a player forgoes the chance of winning the maximum number of tricks and instead aims to ensure the number he requires.

   (1) A Q 7 4 3   (2) A K J 2

        8 6 5 2   8 5 4

In (1), if South needs all five tricks he must finesse the queen, playing West for K x. If he can afford to lose one trick, the safety play is to lay down the ace and then lead up to the queen. This is a precaution against a singleton king in East's hand, for if the queen is finessed and loses to the bare king South will have to lose a second trick.

In (2) the safety play for three tricks is to cash A K, then return to hand to lead up to the J x. This saves the vital trick when East has Q x.

The term is also freely used of many plays that simply represent the best technique, as here:

   (3) A Q 9 6 3   (4) A 9 6 4 2

        K 10 7 2   J 7 3

In (3) the safety play is to cash the ace or queen first, so that if *either* opponent turns up with J x x x he will be open to a marked finesse.

In (4) the best way to make four tricks is to lead low from dummy, playing East for K 10 or Q 10 alone. If East plays an honour, South leads the jack on the next round.

In the wider field of strategy the element of safety enters into most forms of play. The following hand is an example of safety in the development of a suit and in the protection of master cards:

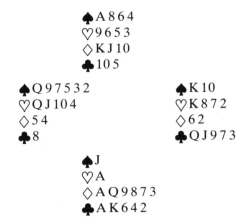

Playing in 6 ◇, South takes the first trick with ♡ A. Clearly he has to develop the clubs and, while it is unlikely that it will make any difference, good technique demands that he cross to dummy with ♠ A for the first lead of clubs. If by any chance East were void, this would prevent the ruff of a master card.

As it is, ♣ A wins, and now comes the critical play: South must lead a low club from his hand. East wins and returns a trump, but there are still two trumps in dummy with which to ruff two club losers.

If South plays off ♣ A K, West will ruff the second round and lead a trump. South will be left with three club losers and only two trumps on the table.

SCISSORS COUP

This is a form of avoidance play in which declarer snips the defenders' only line of communication at an early stage. Often the object is to prevent a defender from obtaining a ruff.

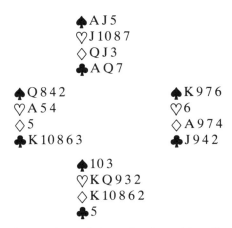

♠A J 5
♡J 10 8 7
◇Q J 3
♣A Q 7

♠Q 8 4 2   ♠K 9 7 6
♡A 5 4   ♡6
◇5   ◇A 9 7 4
♣K 10 8 6 3   ♣J 9 4 2

♠10 3
♡K Q 9 3 2
◇K 10 8 6 2
♣5

South is in 3 ♡ and the defence begins with a diamond lead and diamond ruff. West then leads a small spade.

The defence now threatens to gain a second ruff. If South continues in the normal way, going up with ♠A and leading a trump, West will win with the ace of trumps and put his partner in with a spade for another diamond ruff.

As the cards lie, declarer can avoid this outcome by winning West's spade at trick three and laying down ♣A, followed by ♣Q, on which he discards his losing spade. This has the effect of severing the defenders' only line of communication.

If East were able to cover ♣Q with the king, declarer would have to abandon the coup. He would ruff and lead a second trump, hoping that the defence would not be able to achieve a second ruff.

SIGNALLING

Signalling is the language used by defenders to convey information to one another. A signal is a play made by a defender who is following suit or discarding. The most common example is the *Attitude Signal*, where a defender plays a high card, or high-low, to express encouragement, a low card for discouragement. Special forms of signalling are described under the headings: *Benjamin Trump Signal, Reverse Signals, Roman (Odd-Even) Signals, Smith Peters, Suit-Preference Signals, Trump Echo* and *Vinje Trump Signal.*

SMITH PETERS

This signal for use against notrump contracts was suggested by Mr.
I. G. Smith. When a player wishes his partner to continue the suit
originally led, he echoes in the first suit led by the declarer.

East has the opportunity for a Smith peter in the deal below:

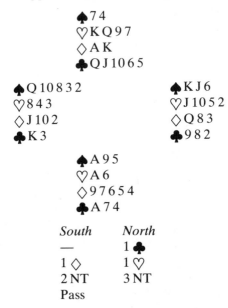

```
                        ♠74
                        ♡KQ97
                        ◇AK
                        ♣QJ1065
        ♠Q10832                    ♠KJ6
        ♡843                       ♡J1052
        ◇J102                      ◇Q83
        ♣K3                        ♣982
                        ♠A95
                        ♡A6
                        ◇97654
                        ♣A74
```

South	North
—	1♣
1◇	1♡
2NT	3NT
Pass	

West leads ♠3 and East plays the king. There is little point in
holding up, so South wins, crosses to a diamond and leads ♣Q. On
this trick East starts an echo with the 9. On winning with the king
West knows that his partner wants a spade continuation.

Smith peters can also be made by the opening leader. As there is
no need to encourage the return of one's own suit, the meaning of an
echo should now be: 'There's no future in my original suit, please
switch to another.'

SMOTHER PLAY

This term describes a rare ending in which life is denied to an apparently certain trump winner held by a defender.

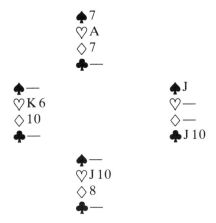

South is playing a heart contract and the lead is in dummy. West, holding K x, with the bare ace on the table, appears to have a sure trump trick, but this vanishes when declarer leads ♠7 from dummy and discards his losing diamond. East has to lead a club. South plays ♡10 and West is left with the choice of under-ruffing uselessly or seeing the king smothered by the ace.

For a different kind of smother play, see *Devil's Coup*.

SQUEEZE PLAY

When a player, usually a defender and usually towards the end of a hand, finds that he cannot discard except at the cost of a trick, he is said to be squeezed. The basis of squeeze play is that two hands may contain between them more vital cards than one opponent can protect. Pressure of space may then compel that opponent to give up his hold on one suit or the other.

In the study of squeeze play, these terms are commonly used:

Squeeze card. In every squeeze you must be able to lead a card to which the opponent cannot follow suit and to which he can discard only at the cost of a trick. This is called the squeeze card.

'Threat' or 'menace' card. A 'threat' is a card that is not a winner but

whose presence obliges at least one opponent to keep a higher card. A squeeze works when one opponent controls two such menaces and cannot keep both when the squeeze card is played.

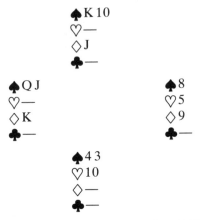

Playing in notrumps, South leads ♡10 and West is squeezed. He must either unguard spades or throw away the winning diamond. Dummy's ♠K 10 are a *two-card menace*—that is, a winner and a loser in the same suit. The jack of diamonds is a *single menace*, and the 10 of hearts is the *squeeze card*.

This is an example of a simple 'one-way' squeeze, where the two-card menace and the single menace are in the same hand, opposite the squeeze card. This type of squeeze works only when both menaces are controlled by the opponent who sits on the left of the squeeze card.

Another essential element is correct timing. West has no 'idle' card that he can throw when the squeeze begins—all his cards are 'busy'.

Special forms of squeeze play are described under the following headings: *Automatic Squeeze, Criss-Cross Squeeze, Defending Against Squeezes, Double Squeeze, Progressive Squeeze, Pseudo-Squeeze, Rectifying the Count, Squeeze Without the Count, Suicide Squeeze, Threat, Trump Squeeze* and *Vienna Coup*.

SQUEEZE WITHOUT THE COUNT

In most squeezes declarer, at the time when the squeeze card is played, is able to win with top cards all the remaining tricks but one, the squeeze providing the extra trick. This, however, is not an invariable condition. There are many variations where a defender wins a trick after the squeeze card has been played; the squeeze may be a preliminary to a throw-in, or to suit establishment. Any such squeeze may be called a 'squeeze without the count'.

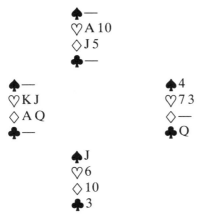

Playing at notrumps, South has only two top winners. He cannot rectify the count for a squeeze, but if he plays his squeeze card now, ♠J, he forces West to part with a diamond. Dummy throws a heart, a diamond is conceded and dummy's ◊J wins the last trick.

In the next example a squeeze prepares the ground for a throw-in.

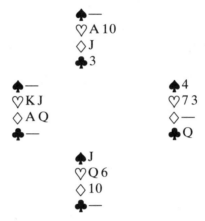

Again the lead of ♠J compels West to give up a diamond winner. He is then thrown in to lead away from ♡K.

SUBMARINE SQUEEZE

See *Rectifying the Count*.

SUICIDE SQUEEZE

When the squeeze card is led by a defender, who thus squeezes his partner, the play is known as a suicide squeeze.

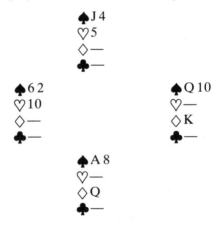

West is on lead, defending against notrumps. If he leads his winning heart he squeezes his partner, who has to discard in front of South. West can save the position by not playing off his winner.

To bring about this type of ending it is often good tactics for declarer in, say, 3 NT, with only eight tricks in view, to return the suit led.

954

A J 7 3 2   Q 8

K 10 6

West leads the 3 and declarer, on winning with the king, returns the suit. West may be able to save the situation, as he can in the first diagram, by not cashing.

There is also the forced suicide squeeze, where declarer exits with a loser and the defender who wins the trick squeezes his partner at the same time. Purists in language have suggested that as the victim is not the player himself but his unfortunate partner, this type of squeeze might more suitably be known as a homicide squeeze. A suicide squeeze, properly so called, occurs in a position such as this:

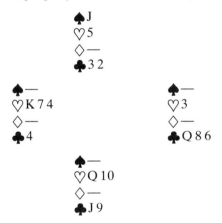

With the lead in dummy, South may cash ♠J, but if he does he subjects himself to a suicidal squeeze and makes no more tricks. By leading a heart or a club instead, he makes two tricks.

Another form of suicide occurs when a defender, as a result of cashing a winner at the wrong moment, rectifies the count for declarer and renders himself open to a subsequent squeeze.

SUIT-PREFERENCE SIGNAL

The special character of this signal, also called McKenney or Lavinthal, is that its message does not relate to the suit in which the signal is made. At a suit contract, the play of an unnecessarily high card is a request for partner to lead the higher ranking of the other two side suits. Thus, when a player leads a card for his partner to ruff, he can indicate by his choice of card which of the two remaining side suits should be returned.

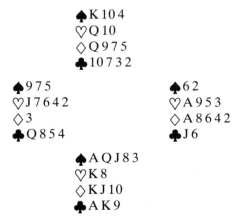

Against 4 ♠, West leads ◇ 3 and East wins. Reading his partner for a single diamond, East returns the 8 for him to ruff. This indicates that his quick entry is in hearts, and West obtains another ruff to set the contract.

This is the simplest form of the signal. Many other uses have been developed. Indeed, almost any card that would otherwise have no significance may be interpreted as a suit-preference signal.

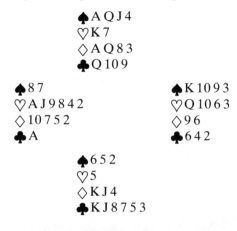

South is in 5 ♣, hearts having been bid by West and supported by East. West starts with ♡ A and East drops the queen to show that he wants a spade shift, not a diamond.

To avoid confusion, most partnerships have an understanding that at the first trick a signal should be suit-preference only when no other sensible meaning can be attached to it.

Sometimes it is possible to issue a suit-preference signal with the opening lead. Suppose you are on lead against 4 ♠ with this hand, having overcalled in clubs and been supported by partner:

♠ 7 2   ♡ 8 3   ♢ K J 10   ♣ K J 9 8 7 2

If you lead ♣ 2 it will be obvious to partner that this is not your lowest card and that your side strength is in diamonds, as opposed to hearts.

A player who has made the opening lead against a notrump contract often has the opportunity to issue a suit-preference signal in the same suit on a later round.

7 4

Q 10 8 5 3   K J 6

A 9 2

West leads the 5 against 3 NT and South holds up his ace until the third round. On the third round West may either play the queen as a suit-preference signal to indicate an entry in a high suit, the 3 to suggest a low suit, or a middle card to express no preference.

The signals are valuable in this type of position also:

10 6 4

A K J 9 3   7 5 2

Q 8

West leads the king of this side suit against a suit contract and East plays the 2, a normal suit-length signal. Knowing it is safe to continue, West lays down the ace. At this trick East may play either the 5 or the 7. The 7 would be a suit-preference signal, indicating values in the higher ranking of the two remaining suits. The 5 would not necessarily be a request for the lowest remaining suit, but there would be a negative inference that East was not especially anxious for the higher suit.

SYMMETRY OF DISTRIBUTION

Many players believe, or half believe, with the authority of Ely Culbertson, that there is a relation between the distribution of their own hands and the distribution of a suit around the table. For example, a player with 5–4–3–1 pattern may be disposed to think that a suit divided 5–4 between himself and dummy is more likely to break 3–1 than the normal probabilities would suggest. That such thinking is illogical can be confirmed by a simple experiment. Imagine a shuffled pack, divided into halves. It is inconceivable that the distributions within one half should affect the distributions within the other half.

TEMPO

This term relates to the element of time in card play, with special reference to the use of opportunities to make an attacking lead. Thus, a player who makes a neutral move when positive action is required is said to 'lose a tempo'.

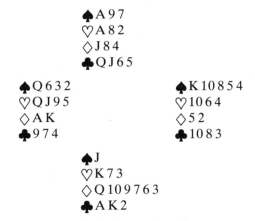

South is playing in 5 ◇, which can be beaten only by repeated heart leads. If West were to lead a top trump, with the idea of having a look at dummy, he would lose a vital tempo: a switch at trick two would be too late.

For the declarer, a special order of play may be needed when control is in the balance and he cannot afford to lose a tempo. For example:

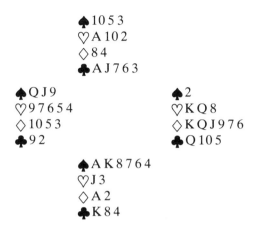

♠ 10 5 3
♡ A 10 2
◇ 8 4
♣ A J 7 6 3

♠ Q J 9
♡ 9 7 6 5 4
◇ 10 5 3
♣ 9 2

♠ 2
♡ K Q 8
◇ K Q J 9 7 6
♣ Q 10 5

♠ A K 8 7 6 4
♡ J 3
◇ A 2
♣ K 8 4

South is in 4 ♠, East having opened with 1 ◇. West leads a diamond and on winning this trick declarer lays down ♠ A K. Faced now with the possibility of a loser in each suit, he plans to establish the clubs for a heart discard.

If South were to cash ♣ K and finesse the jack, he would lose a tempo. East would cash a diamond and return ♡ K. Declining the finesse, South takes three rounds of clubs, setting up a club for a heart discard.

TENACE

A tenace is a combination of cards not in sequence whose trick-winning power depends on how the outstanding cards lie and on who has the lead. In the following diagram North is said to have the major tenace and East the minor tenace:

A Q

x x   K J

x x

A tenace position exists whenever a lead from a favourable quarter will give an extra trick to the side that holds the tenace.

A combination in which the high cards are divided, such as A x opposite Q x, is called a split tenace.

THREAT (OR MENACE)

To execute a squeeze, a player must hold cards in at least two suits that threaten the same opponent. In this diagram East is the player who is threatened.

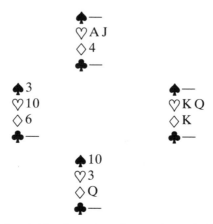

South leads ♠10, throwing dummy's ♢4. East is squeezed because he is threatened by two cards, ♢Q and ♡J. ♢Q is a one-card threat, ♡AJ a two-card threat.

Because of entry requirements, there must always be a two-card threat in the hand opposite the squeeze card. (In the above example, the squeeze card is South's ♠10.) In some variations, however, such as the *Criss-Cross Squeeze*, the two-card threat need not contain a top card.

These are technical terms for various kinds of threat:

Double menace, when a two-card menace headed by a winner is controlled by both opponents. The term (or double-entry menace) is also used for occasions where there is a top card in both hands, K x opposite A x x.

Extended menace, necessary for most forms of progressive squeeze. This occurs when the two-card menace is accompanied by one or more additional low cards which will be winners if the opponent releases his guard.

Isolating the menace, a process whereby a threat originally controlled by both opponents is isolated so that it can be defended by one opponent only. For example, with A K x x opposite x x of a plain suit, declarer ruffs out the third round. Then the last card will be a threat that only one opponent can defend.

Recessed menace, an extended menace headed by two winners, such as A K x opposite a singleton. A recessed threat provides extra space in the hand opposite and may offset what would normally be a poor arrangement of the other menaces.

Split (or divided) menace. When the key cards of a two-card menace are in opposite hands, as in the combination Q x opposite A x, with the opponents K J in between.

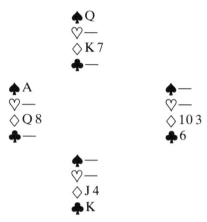

North's diamonds do not, by themselves, represent a two-card menace against West, because East's second diamond is higher than North's 7. But the combined holdings of North and South form a split menace against West. When ♣K is led, West must unguard ◇Q to keep ♠A.

Transferred menace, where control of a menace is transferred from one defender to the other. For example:

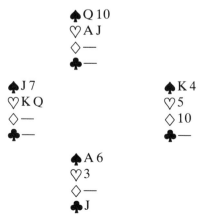

Playing in notrumps with the lead in dummy, declarer leads ♠Q, forcing East to cover with the king. This transfers the spade threat to West, who is squeezed when ♣J is led to the next trick.

THROW-IN

This term describes the situation, usually in the end game, where declarer throws the lead to an opponent who has to play back to a tenace combination. This is the simplest form:

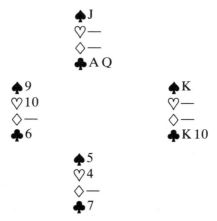

Having reason to place East with both black kings, South exits with a spade and East has to lead into the club tenace.

At notrumps a defender is often thrown in with his own long suit. This is a typical example:

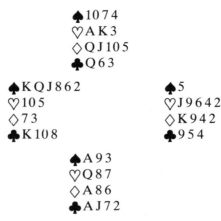

South is in 3 NT, West having overcalled in spades. West leads ♠ K and South captures the second round, East discarding a club. It would be a mistake to hold up for two rounds, for then declarer would have no card of exit with which to throw the lead. To have any chance of nine tricks South must find East with ◇ K, so he crosses to dummy with ♡ K and runs ◇ Q. He continues with ◇ J and then a third diamond to the ace, West throwing a club.

When diamonds fail to split declarer needs two tricks from clubs. He cashes two more hearts, forcing West to make another discard. If West throws a spade, South can place him with exactly three spades and two clubs. He then executes a throw-in by playing a spade, forcing West to lead a club at trick twelve. West may, of course, bare the king of clubs, forcing declarer to a guess.

TOP-OF-NOTHING LEAD

When a player leads his highest card from three or more spot cards, he is said to lead 'top-of-nothing'.

Lead from three small

Top-of-nothing is the traditional lead from a combination such as 8 5 4 (although *MUD* has a significant following). It is the custom in America to play the middle card on the second round, but there is no technical disadvantage in playing the lowest. Whether partner will be able to distinguish between a doubleton and three small depends on the rank of the intervening cards.

Lead from four or more small

Against a trump contract the general practice is to lead top-of-nothing in the case of an unbid suit, but to lead fourth best in the case of partner's suit. When the leader has supported his partner's suit, however, the choice is again top-of-nothing.

Against a notrump contract, fourth best is normal. Only from such a sequence as 9 8 7 x x would top-of-nothing be led. Another idea is to lead 'second from the top' of poor suits, the 7 from 9 7 4 2 or 9 7 5 3 2.

TRUMP CONTROL

When declarer can draw the opposing trumps and retain sufficient trumps to develop his side suits, he is said to possess trump control.

There are many tactical moves open to a declarer who is threatened with loss of trump control. One rests on his timing in the trump suit itself:

♠ 8 4
♡ 10 7 3 2
◇ A K
♣ Q J 7 3 2

♠ A K J 10 6
♡ 5
◇ 10 7 4 3
♣ A K 6

Hearts are led against South's 4 ♠ contract and he has to ruff the second round. If he enters dummy with a diamond in order to finesse spades, he may lose control. Say that West wins and plays another heart: South ruffs again, but he has now been shortened twice and if the trumps were originally 4–2 he will not be able to draw them.

The safe play for ten tricks, after ruffing the second lead, is to lay down the ace and king of trumps and then, if the queen does not fall, play clubs. The opponents will make two trump tricks, but that will be all against any normal break.

Another move in the battle for trump control is to refuse to ruff until dummy is void in the suit that is being attacked.

♠ J 7
♡ 7 5 4
◇ K Q 8 6 2
♣ 10 5 4

♠ A K Q 10 6
♡ 10 3
◇ J 10 5
♣ A K 6

Against 3 ♠ the defence begins with three rounds of hearts. If South ruffs and draws trumps he will be in difficulties if the spades are 4–2, for the ace of diamonds will still be out. A possible plan is to ruff the third heart and force out ◇ A while dummy still has a trump with which to deal with another heart lead. The danger in this is that the opponents may be able to hold up ♢ A for one round and collect a diamond ruff.

The safest play is to throw the losing club on the third round of hearts, loser-on-loser play. The contract will then be safe unless the opponents take an immediate diamond ruff. That is not likely, for had there been a singleton they would probably have led the suit earlier.

TRUMP COUP

There are many coups that centre round the trump suit, but the term 'trump coup' is used especially of the following kind of end position:

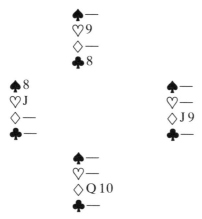

Diamonds are trumps and if South is on lead he has to lose a trick. With dummy on lead, however, declarer brings off a trump coup to take both tricks. In effect, he takes a trump finesse against East though dummy has no trump to lead. That is the essence of the trump coup.

It is usually when the trumps break badly that declarer has to play for a trump coup. The above ending results from the following hand:

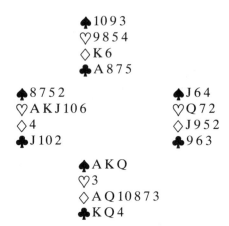

♠1093
♡9854
◇K6
♣A875

♠8752   ♠J64
♡AKJ106   ♡Q72
◇4   ◇J952
♣J102   ♣963

♠AKQ
♡3
◇AQ10873
♣KQ4

South is in 6 ◇ and West leads ♡ A K, South ruffing. As he may need all entries to dummy for trump reduction, South plays ◇ A and ◇ K. Discovering the break, he ruffs a heart, then cashes three spades and three clubs to arrive at the position shown above.

South is lucky to find that East follows suit in both black suits. Note, however, that West's lead of a second heart at trick two assisted the declarer's plan.

See also *Grand Coup* and, for other coups in the trump suit, *Coup en Passant, Devil's Coup*, and *Smother Play*.

TRUMP ECHO

An echo in the trump suit shows not a doubleton, as in a plain suit, but a tripleton. This is because it might be imprudent to echo with such a holding as 10 x or 9 x.

The echo can be employed in a general way to give partner a count. Thus if the declarer with a solid trump suit lays down the A K Q it costs nothing to echo with three small trumps and may help partner to count the hand.

There are other situations where a defender whose partner is about to win a trump trick must use his judgement whether to echo or not. If he has expectations of a ruff he will echo, but if he has no such expectation it may be wise to refrain from the echo, directing partner's attention to a different suit from the one where a ruff might be possible.

TRUMP PROMOTION

A trump promotion occurs when the defenders create extra trump tricks by a tactical manoeuvre. One common example is the *Uppercut*. The other effective method of trump promotion is to lead a plain suit through declarer, who has to ruff in front of the other defender.

$$6\,2$$

$$J\,7\,4 \qquad\qquad 8\,5$$

$$A\,K\,Q\,10\,9\,3$$

If this is the trump suit declarer will lose a trick when East leads a plain suit of which both South and West are void.

Often, however, the extra trick is created by refusal to over-ruff, as here:

$$8\,5\,4$$

$$A\,10\,2 \qquad\qquad 6\,3$$

$$K\,Q\,J\,9\,7$$

This is the trump suit and East leads a plain suit. When South ruffs high, West can ensure two trump tricks by declining to over-ruff.

There are innumerable variations of this theme. Even when the prospect of a trump promotion is not obvious, a defender should be guided by the principle that it is usually wrong to over-ruff when holding a sure trump winner. For example:

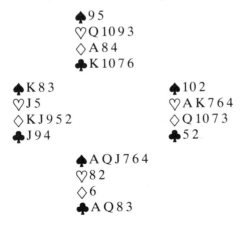

♠9 5
♡Q 10 9 3
◇A 8 4
♣K 10 7 6

♠K 8 3   ♠10 2
♡J 5   ♡A K 7 6 4
◇K J 9 5 2   ◇Q 10 7 3
♣J 9 4   ♣5 2

♠A Q J 7 6 4
♡8 2
◇6
♣A Q 8 3

The contract is 4 ♠ and West leads ♡J, which is covered by the queen and king. East plays ace and another heart and declarer ruffs with the queen of trumps. Though the prospect of a second trump trick is uncertain, it cannot profit West to over-ruff, so he discards. When partner turns up with the 10, West collects two trump tricks.

TRUMP SQUEEZE

In a trump squeeze an opponent who has the top control of a suit is forced to reduce his holding so that his winner can be ruffed out.

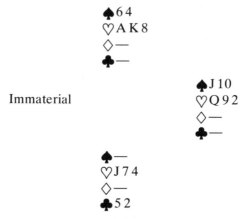

Clubs are trumps and the next to last trump, as is usual in this type of squeeze, begins the operation. Dummy throws a heart and East is lost: if he discards a spade, dummy's second spade can be established. The position resembles a criss-cross squeeze, a trump serving as the second top control.

Two quick entries to the hand opposite the squeeze card are essential in all trump squeezes. In the diagram above, the second entry is in the suit of the two-card menace. Here it lies in a third suit:

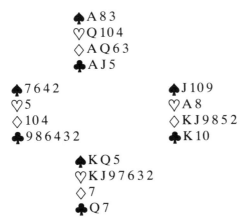

South plays in 6♡ after East has opened 1◇. He wins the diamond lead in dummy, forces out ♡A, and plays for this ending:

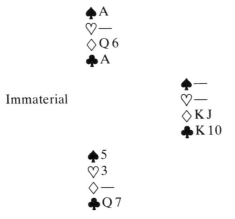

A spade to the ace (the vital second entry) squeezes East.

TWO-WAY FINESSE

This is a finesse that can be taken against either opponent. Usually, a queen or jack is the missing card.

(1)   A J x x   (2)   K 10 x

    K 10 9   Q 9 x

In each case South may play either opponent for the vital card.

There are also many combinations where a finesse may be taken in either direction but where particular play offers the better percentage chance. For example:

(3)   K x x   (4) K 10 x x

      A J 10 x x   Q 9 7 x

In (3), by playing the king first and then finessing the jack, declarer can pick up Q 9 x x in East's hand. If the ace were played first he would not be able to pick up this combination in either hand.

In (4) the question is whether to lead first towards the king or the queen. Leading up to the king is better because on the next round South intends to lead the 10, picking up a possible A J 8 x in the East hand.

UNBLOCKING PLAY

This common stratagem consists of the play of an unnecessarily high card for various reasons, such as to facilitate the run of a suit, to prepare for a finesse, or to escape the lead. These are some examples of unblocking in the end game:

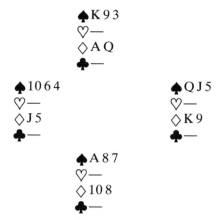

When South, requiring the last four tricks at notrumps, plays off ♠A and ♠K, East must unblock the queen and jack to avoid being thrown in.

Here West is made the victim of a ruff-and-discard elimination unless he unblocks:

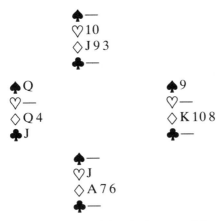

Hearts are trumps and South leads the ace of diamonds. To avoid being end-played, West must unblock by playing the queen.

In the next example the declarer must unblock a winning card in the dummy to effect a progressive squeeze:

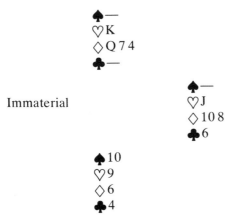

Needing all four tricks at notrumps, South leads the 10 of spades. If a diamond is thrown from dummy, East can defend the position by discarding a heart. Instead, South must throw ♡K from dummy. Then East has no good discard.

UPPERCUT

This term for a certain kind of trump promotion is apt because the fatal blow comes from below. In the hope of promoting his partner's trumps, a defender ruffs as high as he can, though he expects to be over-ruffed.

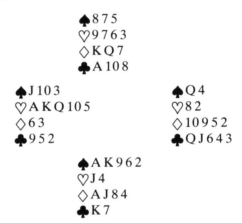

The contract is 4 ♠ and West leads out three rounds of hearts. If East ruffs the third round with the queen, declarer must lose two trump tricks. To make sure that his partner will ruff high, West can lead a low heart on the third round. East will then realize what is expected of him.

In the following example the uppercut strikes the dummy:

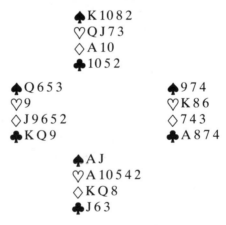

Against 4 ♡ West leads K Q and another club. East wins and judges that the setting trick can come only from trumps, so he plays the thirteenth club. West uppercuts with ♡9, forcing the jack from dummy and leaving East with a certain trump trick.

VIENNA COUP

This is an unblocking play that is sometimes necessary before declarer can benefit from a squeeze position.

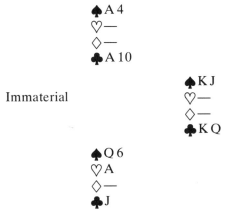

Declarer has the material for a squeeze against East, who has to guard both spades and clubs. However, if declarer lays down ♡A, discarding a spade from dummy, East too will discard a spade and declarer will not benefit because the spades will be blocked.

Declarer must play off ♠A at an earlier point, unblocking the suit. Then, in the three-card ending, East will be squeezed.

In technical terms, the Vienna Coup consists of the play of the top-ranking card of a suit so that a card of lower rank in the opposite hand will be correctly positioned as a one-card threat in an automatic squeeze.

VINJE TRUMP SIGNAL

The traditional signal by defenders in the trump suit (see *Trump Echo*) is of limited usefulness, as defenders can often tell the length of declarer's trump suit from the bidding. A different scheme has been propounded by Helge Vinge, of Norway.

A hand of 13 cards is bound to consist of either:

(*a*) One suit with an even number of cards and three suits with an odd number of cards; or

(*b*) One suit with an odd number of cards and three suits with an even number. (A void counts as an even number.) *A hand will always contain 'parity' types in a proportion of 1:3.*

The Vinje Trump Signal indicates the make-up of the defender's hand as follows:

(*a*) High-low shows that the hand has one suit with an even number of cards, three suits with an odd number of cards.

(*b*) Low-high shows that the hand has one suit with an odd number of cards, three suits with an even number of cards.

The other defender, armed with this information, can tell the 'parity' type held both by his partner and by declarer as soon as he knows the one suit that is even or the one suit that is odd. Helge Vinje gives this example:

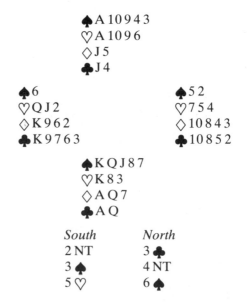

♠A 10 9 4 3
♡A 10 9 6
♢J 5
♣J 4

♠6   ♠5 2
♡Q J 2   ♡7 5 4
♢K 9 6 2 ♢10 8 4 3
♣K 9 7 6 3 ♣10 8 5 2

♠K Q J 8 7
♡K 8 3
♢A Q 7
♣A Q

South	North
2 NT	3 ♣
3 ♠	4 NT
5 ♡	6 ♠

West leads ♠6 and declarer takes a second round of this suit. West discards a club and East, using the Vinje Trump Signal, follows suit in the order 2 5, indicating a hand pattern of one suit with an odd number of cards. Declarer continues with three rounds of hearts, throwing West into the lead. What should West return, clubs or diamonds?

The trump signal provides the answer. East has indicated one suit with an odd number of cards, and this is now seen to be hearts, in which he has followed three times. East therefore has an even number of spades, diamonds and clubs. West can safely exit with a club and wait for his diamond trick.

WAITING MOVE

In bridge, though much less frequently than in chess, the player's best move may be to avoid committing himself in any positive direction. This is a standard example:

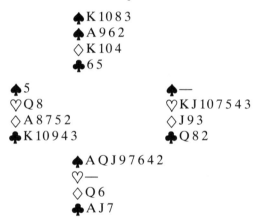

```
            ♠K 10 8 3
            ♠A 9 6 2
            ◇K 10 4
            ♣6 5

♠5                        ♠—
♡Q 8                      ♡K J 10 7 5 4 3
◇A 8 7 5 2                ◇J 9 3
♣K 10 9 4 3              ♣Q 8 2

            ♠A Q J 9 7 6 4 2
            ♡—
            ◇Q 6
            ♣A J 7
```

South plays in 6 ♠ after East has opened with a pre-emptive bid of 3 ♡. West leads ♡Q. If declarer discards a club on ♡A and relies on a finesse of ◇10 for his second discard, he will fail. He must ruff the opening lead, play a round of trumps, and follow with a low diamond from hand. This places West in a dilemma. If he ducks, he allows South to dispose of ◇Q on ♡A, and if he goes up with ◇A he provides declarer with two discards, one on ♡A and one on ◇K.

For a distinctive appellation of the dilemma created by the lead of ◇6, see *Morton's Fork*.

Part 3

LAWS, TOURNAMENT PROCEDURE and DEFINITIONS

ALERT PROCEDURE

Players at both rubber bridge and duplicate have a duty to warn opponents of any conventional call or play that may not be fully understood. At rubber bridge, where the use of conventions is often restricted, either the conventions must be described in advance or notice may be given of the intention to use conventions of which a full explanation may be deferred until occasion arises.

At duplicate there is a full-scale alert procedure. Thus, when a player opens with, say, a conventional one club, his partner must tap the table to warn the next player that the bid has a special meaning, about which he may wish to enquire. (In America, instead of tapping, the player announces, 'Alert'.) Failure to alert, in tournament play, may lead to a penalty or an adjusted score. Certain very familiar conventions may be classified by the sponsoring organization as 'non-alertable'.

Should partner, when asked to explain a convention, give a wrong answer, this may give grounds for an adjusted score. Nevertheless, he should not be corrected. In the same way, if a player, by the operation of the Alert procedure, realizes that he has made the wrong bid in the system, he must not take advantage. For example, South bids 1 NT, thinking he is playing a weak notrump, North informs the opponents (correctly) that his side is playing a strong notrump and bids 4 NT. In such case South is exhorted to continue as though he had not received the new information: he must bid as though North had bid 4 NT over a weak notrump.

See also *Skip Bid.*

AMERICAN WHIST MOVEMENT

This is one of the simplest and most useful movements for a multiple team-of-four contest. It can be used for any odd number of teams.

Suppose there are seven teams playing four-board matches against one another. To begin, the players sit as complete teams at tables one to seven and a set of boards is placed on each table; boards one to four on table one, five to eight on table two, and so on.

For the first round, the North–South pairs remain at their tables and the East–West pairs move two tables down, from five to three, from three to one, from one to six. The boards are moved one table down in the same way, from five to four and so on. The same movement is repeated for each of the six rounds of the tournament.

Each team will meet each other team over the same set of boards, but play will not be simultaneous, as it is in the Patton movement. Thus, no comparison of scores is permissible until the end of the contest.

It will be observed that, although 28 boards are required for a seven-team tournament, each team plays only 24 boards, missing the set that is placed on its table at the start of the movement.

When there is an even number of tables, the most satisfactory solution is the 'Stagger' movement.

'Stagger' movement for an even number of tables

The tables are set in two parallel rows. Thus with ten teams, tables 1 to 5 are set parallel with 6 to 10. There will be ten sets of three boards in play. The session is played in two halves, only boards 1 to 15 being required at first.

Each team takes its place at a table and takes its team number there. For the first round the East–West pair moves down one table and plays the boards on that table. Thereafter the movement is similar to an American Whist movement: the East–West pairs move down two tables, leaving the boards on the intervening table.

Boards are shared between parallel tables, 1 with 6, 2 with 7, and so on. When the first half-session is completed the players may compare scores. The movement for the second half is the same as for the first.

BID

In terms of the Laws, a bid is an undertaking to win tricks. The comprehensive term, call, includes pass, double and redouble.

BIDDING BOXES

Invented by a Swedish engineer, Gosta Nordeenson, these permit silent bidding. A box of indexed cards is clamped to each player's corner of the table. All the cards remain on the table until the bidding is over, thus obviating the need for any review.

One obvious advantage is that language (and audibility) problems are avoided. Bidding boxes are preferred by nearly all tournament players who have experienced their use. In Scandinavia their use is widespread and in World Bridge Federation tournaments they are compulsory. Obviously they make it much easier for spectators to follow the proceedings.

BID OUT OF TURN

The penalty varies according to circumstances.

	(Dealer)			
(1)	*South*	*West*	*North*	*East*
				1 ♡

This is a bid out of turn before anyone has called. The bidding reverts to South and West must pass throughout. East may call as he chooses.

	(Dealer)			
(2)	*South*	*West*	*South*	*East*
	Pass			1 ♡

This is a bid out of turn after someone has called and when it was the turn of the offender's partner. West must pass throughout and if West becomes the opening leader the declarer may require or prohibit the lead of a specified suit. (*In this and all similar cases the prohibition extends so long as the player retains the lead.*)

	(Dealer)			
(3)	*South*	*West*	*North*	*East*
	1 ◇	1 ♡		1 ♠

Here East has bid out of turn after someone has called and when it was the turn of his right-hand opponent. The bidding reverts to North. If North passes, East must repeat his bid of one spade and there is no penalty. If North makes any other call, East may call as he chooses and West must pass throughout.

Duplicate Law

1. There is a special case where the second hand is the offender. Suppose North is the dealer and East bids out of turn. Now, if North passes, East must repeat his bid and there is no penalty; if North bids, then if East makes a bid in the same denomination as before, West must pass for one round, but if East acts otherwise West must pass throughout. Also, there may be a lead penalty if East, on this round, bids a different denomination from before: if the first bid was a suit, then declarer may require or forbid a lead of that suit when the offender's partner first has the lead; if the first bid was in notrumps, declarer may require the lead of a specified suit.

2. If East bids out of turn before any player has called and when it was the turn of South or West, the bidding reverts and West must pass throughout; there may also be a lead penalty in the circumstances described in the preceding paragraph.

3. If East bids out of turn after any player has called when it was the turn of his partner to call, West must pass throughout and if West has the opening lead declarer may require or forbid the lead of a specified suit.

4. East bids out of turn after any player has called and when it was North's turn; now, if North passes, East must repeat his bid and there is no penalty; if North makes any legal call other than a pass and East then bids in the same denomination as before, West must pass for one round, but if East takes any other action West must pass throughout and there may be a lead penalty in the circumstances described under 1 above.

BOARD-A-MATCH SCORING

This method of scoring used to be standard in North America for multiple team contests. Each board has the value of one match point and the side that wins the board, whether by 10 points or 2,000, scores one point, the losers 0. When the result is a tie, each team scores half a point.

Bidding and play under these conditions is extremely keen. Players will take considerable risks in contesting a part-score and borderline doubles are frequent. There is emphasis on play in no-trumps, because of the extra 10 points, and a declarer will freely risk his contract for an extra trick. (In British tournaments a difference of 10 in constructive contracts, e.g. 120 for 2 NT against 110 for 2 ♠, counts as a tie.)

Board-a-match scoring has been largely superseded in North America by Swiss team events scored by *International Match Points* (I.M.P.s). In Britain and France board-a-match scoring is sometimes combined with I.M.P. in multiple events. In a three-board match, for example, a total of 10 points is at stake, divided as follows: 2 points for winning the board (1 each for a tie); 4 points on the basis of aggregate score, according to the difference in totals:

Difference of	Divide
0–240	2–2
250–490	3–1
500 and over	4–0

Slightly different scales can be devised for longer matches. This form of scoring is sometimes known as Hybrid Scoring.

BRIDGERAMA

Devised in Italy and first used in the 1958 World Championship, this is a large electric display board for showing bridge, usually match play, to an audience. It shows not only the play of each card but also the bidding, the vulnerability, and so on. In operation it requires a large staff and since the early 1970s the use of *Vu-Graph* has been much more common. Both types of presentation can be enhanced by showing the players on closed-circuit television.

BUTLER METHOD

This is a method of scoring a pairs event in terms of *International Match Points*. The scores of all competing pairs on a board are totalled and divided to provide an average or 'datum'. Thus the datum for North-South may be, say, +370 on a board where game has sometimes been made, sometimes not. When the field is fairly large, the top and bottom scores may be eliminated from this calculation, to limit the effect of freakish results. Each pair obtains a score in I.M.P.s by comparing its own score with the datum. When two pairs have met over a series of boards there may be a conversion into victory points.

CALL OUT OF TURN

See *Bid out of Turn, Double or Redouble out of Turn, Pass out of Turn*.

CHANGING A CALL

Correction of a misnomer carries no penalty when made without pause. When not so made, the second call is cancelled and:
(*a*) When the first call was illegal the second call is ignored and the player pays the penalty for the first, illegal call.
(*b*) When the first call was legal, the player may either stay with his first call, in which case his partner must pass for one round, or he may make any other legal call, in which case his partner must pass

throughout. If the offender changes the denomination, declarer may prohibit the offender's partner from leading the first suit or, if the bid was in notrumps, may require the offender's partner to lead a specified suit.

Duplicate Law

Same, except that when the first call was illegal it must stand. If the cancelled call was of a different denomination declarer may require or forbid the lead of this suit when the offender's partner first obtains the lead; or, if the cancelled call was in notrumps, may require the lead of a specified suit.

CHICAGO

Popular in America, this is in effect four-deal rubber bridge. It avoids long rubbers of uncertain duration and provides a keen game in which the tactics do not differ greatly from ordinary rubber bridge, except that the value of a part-score is less, as the chance to convert it soon expires.

On the first deal neither side is vulnerable. On the second and third deals, the dealer's side is vulnerable. (This is the normal practice in North America, where 'Chicago' originated, but the alternative method—dealer's side not vulnerable—makes for livelier bidding.) On the fourth deal both sides are vulnerable.

There is a game bonus of 300 or 500 points, according to vulnerability, for each game made during the chukker. Slam bonuses are normal. A passed-out deal does not count and the same player redeals.

A part score may be added to a part score made previously (unless it has been cancelled by a game made by either side). The game bonus then depends on the vulnerability at the time the game is completed. There is a bonus of 100 points for a part score in the fourth deal, but at no other time.

Because of the higher game and slam bonuses it is an advantage to be vulnerable. Therefore, a player who is not vulnerable against vulnerable opponents should incline to open light in third and fourth hand, to prevent a redeal with the same vulnerability.

CLAIM OR CONCESSION BY DECLARER

When declarer makes a claim or concession, either by word or gesture, either defender may ask for all the cards to be exposed and may require declarer to amplify his statement. If asked to play on, declarer must leave his cards face up, must play according to his statement, and may not make any unannounced play (notably a finesse) whose success depends on the lie of the cards. If he attempts to do so, defenders may either accept or forbid the card played. Declarer may, however, take a finesse that was marked before the claim, an opponent having shown out in the suit.

A concession is inoperative if declarer concedes a trick that could not be lost by *any* play of the cards or concedes a contract he has already fulfilled.

Duplicate Law

If declarer's claim is contested, the tournament director must be summoned. Having heard the facts and examined the cards, he will make an equitable decision. If there is a trump outstanding and there is any (not wholly irrational) possibility that declarer might have lost a trick to this trump, the trick will be awarded to the defenders.

CLAIM OR CONCESSION BY DEFENDER

A defender who wishes to make a claim or concession may best do so by showing his cards to the declarer only. If he makes any statement or shows cards to his partner, he may be subject to the penalties for exposing his cards. In this case the declarer may call cards from the other defender.

A concession is inoperative if a defender concedes a trick that could not be lost by *any* play of the cards or concedes a contract he has already defeated. A concession by one defender is not binding if the other defender immediately questions it.

Duplicate Law

If a defender's claim is contested, the tournament director must be summoned. In making his decision he will award any doubtful trick to the declarer.

CONDONING IMPROPER CALL OR PLAY

It is open to a player, and is in no way unethical, to condone an illegal call, play or lead by an opponent. He does this by calling or playing in normal sequence. The illegal call or play is thereby condoned and bidding or play continues as though there had been no infraction. (At rubber bridge, though not at duplicate, this must be done before attention has been drawn to the illegal call, for drawing attention cancels the call and invokes the penalty provisions.) In the event of an 'impossible' call, however, the player is deemed to have passed.

CONVENTION CARD

In duplicate it is common for players to carry a card showing all the partnership conventions in concise form. Often this is on one side of the private score-card used for recording the results.

CONVENTIONS IN TOURNAMENT PLAY

As explained under *Alert Procedure*, players have a duty to advise opponents whenever a conventional call or play is made that may not be understood or expected. A player may always depart from a convention, whether a general understanding such as 'strong no-trump' or a fairly rigid convention such as *Blackwood*, provided his partner be not aware of what is happening.

DEFECTIVE TRICK

A player who has failed to play to a trick or who has played more than one card must correct the error if discovered before both sides have played a card to the next trick. Ownership of the trick goes by the normal rules (but after such correction, the non-offending side may change its own play). A card withdrawn by the offender becomes a penalty card.

If the error is discovered too late, ownership of the trick must stand. The player with too many cards forthwith contributes a card to the defective trick; a player who is short does not play to the final trick or tricks. A player who has mislaid a card is subject to revoke penalties.

Duplicate Law

A player who has failed to play to a previous trick or tricks and has not corrected in time plays on with too many cards, and at the end of play such cards are added to the defective tricks without change of ownership.

When the defective trick cannot be rectified in time, the play of too many or too few cards is penalized as an established revoke.

DOUBLE OR REDOUBLE OUT OF TURN

When the double or redouble would be legal (not *Inadmissible*) if not out of turn, the penalty depends on whose proper turn it was.

South	West	North	East
1 ♡	1 ♠	2 ◇	Pass
4 ♡			Double

Here East has doubled when it was West's turn. West must pass throughout; East may not double four hearts if this comes round to him; and if South is the eventual declarer he may require or forbid the lead by West of a specified suit.

South	West	North	East
1 ♡	Pass	2 ♡	2 NT
Double	Pass		Redouble

East has redoubled when it was the turn of his right-hand opponent. If North passes, the redouble must be repeated and there is no penalty. If North makes any legal call, East may take any action he chooses and West must pass on the next round.

Duplicate Law

Should the offender change denomination on this round, there may be a lead penalty as described under *Changing a Call* (Duplicate Law).

DRAW FOR PARTNERS

A player who draws one of the four cards at the end of the pack, or a card adjoining the card drawn by another player or a card from a different pack, must draw again. It is incorrect to turn the card drawn until all players have drawn.

DUMMY'S RIGHTS

Dummy may give information about fact or law or warn against an irregularity such as leading from the wrong hand. He forfeits his rights, however, if he has looked at his partner's cards or, uninvited, at an opponent's hand. In such case, if he is first to draw attention to an opponent's irregularity, or to warn partner against an irregularity, his side loses its rights. If he warns declarer of a revoke, this must still be corrected but is penalized as an established revoke.

If dummy improperly suggests the play of a card or suit from dummy, either defender may require that such card, or its equivalent, be played or not played.

Duplicate Law

Dummy's rights and limitations are more closely defined and the penalties are stricter. One difference is that dummy may not call attention to irregularities during play, except to prevent one. Nor may he call the tournament director during play.

DUPLICATE SCORING

In duplicate bridge the scoring for odd tricks, doubled and re-doubled contracts, and slam bonuses, is the same as in rubber bridge. Each hand however is scored as a separate event. The vulnerability is indicated on the 'duplicate board' that contains the cards. There is no carrying forward of part scores and no rubber to be completed. Special bonuses are assigned to part-score and game contracts, as follows:

50-point bonus for bidding and making any part-score, whether vulnerable or not;
300-point bonus for bidding and making a non-vulnerable game;
500-point bonus for bidding and making a vulnerable game.
Honours do not count in duplicate.

ETHICS

Broadly speaking, ethics are concerned with what is fair, *Proprieties* with what is mannerly. Certain ethical points are mentioned under *Alert Procedure, Conventions* and *Skip Bid*. Leaving aside such obviously unfair practices as calling or playing with special emphasis or inflexion or timing that may convey a message to partner or may be calculated to deceive an opponent, these are some situations where doubt may exist.

It is not wrong to hesitate, nor to hesitate and pass (though this should if possible be avoided), and the frequent remark, 'I had to bid because I had hesitated', is based on a misconception of the ethical point involved. What is wrong is for the partner of the player who has hesitated (or who has bid more hastily than usual) to draw an inference therefrom and act on it. In tournaments a player may have to satisfy the director not merely that the action he has taken was reasonable and correct in his own eyes but that any tournament player would probably have done the same thing.

It is not wrong to draw an inference from an opponent's hesitation or mannerism, but a player does so at his own risk. If it turns out that he has drawn the wrong conclusion he has no redress.

The fact that an irregularity carries no penalty does not mean that a player is ethically free to commit it. For example, if declarer plays from dummy before the left-hand opponent has played, fourth hand cannot be penalized if he plays out of turn, but he should not deliberately do so.

There is no obligation to call attention to an infraction by one's own side, but no unnatural action should be taken to conceal the offence.

It is improper to infringe a Law deliberately. It is, however, never wrong to condone an opponent's improper call, lead or play, for one's own tactical advantage.

It is sharp practice to watch for the place in his hand from which a player draws a card and to draw an inference therefrom.

It is wrong to draw attention to the score after all players have picked up their cards, and wrong, during the play, to draw attention to the number of tricks won or lost. (At duplicate, however, either dummy or a defender may draw attention to a trick that has been wrongly 'pointed'.) It is incorrect to demand a review of the auction, or an inspection of a trick, for partner's benefit.

It is never ethically wrong to enforce a legal penalty and the proprieties recommend that this be consistently done. (A penalty may, of course, be waived if any unnecessary word or action by the non-offending side may have contributed to it.)

EXPOSED CARD

There is no penalty for exposing a single spot card during the auction. In the case of an honour card, or more than one card, or the exposure with intent to lead of any card, the partner must pass at his next turn and such cards become penalty cards. For exposed cards during the play, see *Penalty Card*.

EXPOSED HAND

For the situation where declarer exposes his hand after a lead out of turn, see *Lead out of Turn*.

If a defender exposes his hand or any part of it, otherwise than after declarer's claim or concession, each such card becomes a *Penalty Card*; except that after a defender's claim or concession declarer may treat the cards of the *other* defender as penalty cards.

GOULASH

For a Goulash, the cards are not shuffled in the ordinary way. They are dealt in a manner likely to produce freakish distribution.

A Goulash generally follows a throw-in or a hand where the bidding has ended in a tame part score. If the players agree, the part score is conceded, and instead of mixing the cards together the players sort their hands according to suits and rank. The pack is cut once and dealt in batches of 5–5–3. The resulting hands are usually, but not always, freakish.

Goulashes are not provided for in the Laws but are, in fact, played at London's Portland Club, one of the bodies responsible for the Laws of Bridge.

HOWELL MOVEMENT

This is a movement for a pairs tournament in which each pair plays an equal number of boards against each other pair. It differs in that respect from the standard form of *Mitchell Movement*, in which a pair sits North–South or East–West throughout and plays against only half the other pairs.

In a Howell movement each pair (except one pivot pair) circulates in accordance with the instructions on its guide card, playing sometimes North–South and sometimes East–West.

A Howell movement can be designed for any number of pairs but cannot be improvised. The tournament director must know the movement and guide cards must be available to the players. The Howell movement has the advantage of producing one winner from the field.

IMPROPER CALL

The term covers infrequent and irregular calls, aside from normal infringements.

A bid, double or redouble by a player who is required to pass is cancelled and his side must pass for the remainder of the bidding. If the offender's partner has the opening lead, declarer may require or forbid the lead of a specified suit.

If a player of the defending side bids, doubles or redoubles after the auction has been closed, declarer may require the offender's partner, when first he gains the lead, to lead or refrain from leading a specified suit.

See also *Inadmissible Double or Redouble.*

IMPROPER REMARK

See *Unauthorized Information.*

INADMISSIBLE DOUBLE OR REDOUBLE

An 'impossible' double or redouble of any sort is cancelled. Two cases then arise:

1.	*South*	*West*	*North*	*East*
	3 ♡	Double	Pass	Double

Here East has doubled a bid that his partner has already doubled. (It is the same if he redoubles a bid already redoubled.) East may pass now; West must pass throughout, either member of the opposing side may cancel all previous doubles or redoubles, and West may be prohibited from leading a heart (the suit illegally doubled). Alternatively, East may substitute a legal bid; again West must pass throughout and may be forbidden to lead a heart.

2. In all other situations the offender must make a legal call and his partner must pass throughout.

Duplicate Law

Any impossible double or redouble is cancelled. The offender may substitute any legal call. (If he bids in a new denomination on this round, his partner, on the opening lead, may be required or forbidden to lead a specified suit.) If the bid improperly doubled (or redoubled) becomes the final contract, either member of the non-offending side may require that it be played undoubled.

INDIVIDUAL TOURNAMENT

This is a duplicate tournament in which each competitor plays an equal number of boards in partnership with each other competitor. The results on each board are match-pointed as in a pairs tournament, each player carrying forward his score on an individual basis.

As a test of skill, individual tournaments are less highly regarded than other forms of duplicate contest.

INSPECTION OF TRICKS

Any player may inspect a trick until he or his partner has led or played to the next trick. Otherwise, a trick may be inspected before the end of play only if there is doubt whether it contained the correct number of cards.

Duplicate Law

A player may inspect the previous trick only if his own card is still face up and his side has not led or played to the next trick. Otherwise, tricks may be inspected only at the director's instruction.

INSUFFICIENT BID

An insufficient bid, if not corrected without pause, becomes subject to penalty and must be corrected by a pass or bid. It may not be corrected by a double or redouble. The penalty depends on the nature of the correction:

South	West	North	East
2 ♠	2 ◇		

Now, (1) if West makes the lowest sufficient bid in the same denomination by bidding three diamonds, there is no penalty; (2) if West makes any other bid, East must pass throughout; (3) if West passes, East must pass throughout and if East becomes the eventual leader he may be required or forbidden to lead a specified suit; (4) if West improperly seeks to amend to a double (or redouble) he is deemed to have passed and incurs the penalty described under (3).

Duplicate Law

Same, except that when the correction is in a different denomination there may in addition be a lead penalty, as described in *Changing a Call* (Duplicate Law).

INTERNATIONAL MATCH POINTS

Invented in Europe, this is now the almost universal method of scoring duplicate matches between teams of four. (See *Match Play*.)

The result of each board is taken separately and the net swing (in terms of total points) between the two teams is converted to I.M.P.s in accordance with the following scale.

Difference on board	*I.M.P.s*	*Difference on board*	*I.M.P.s*
0–10	0	700–790	13
20–40	1	800–890	14
50–80	2	900–1040	15
90–120	3	1050–1190	16
130–160	4	1200–1340	17
170–210	5	1350–1490	18
220–260	6	1500–1740	19
270–310	7	1750–1990	20
320–360	8	2000–2240	21
370–420	9	2250–2490	22
430–490	10	2500–2990	23
500–590	11	3000–3490	24
600–690	12	3500 and up	25

Thus, if a vulnerable contract of 4 ♡ is defeated at one table and made at the other table, the net swing is 720 points, which is converted to 13 I.M.P.s. One team, therefore, scores +13 I.M.P.s while its opponents score −13 I.M.P.s.

The effect of I.M.P. scoring, as opposed to total points, is that part-score hands have more importance. Thus there is a greater premium on skill, as two or three swings on small hands will cancel out a possibly lucky slam swing.

LAWS OF BRIDGE

The 1963 code for rubber bridge is promulgated by the National Laws Commission of the American Contract Bridge League, the Card Committee of the Portland Club, and the European Bridge League. The 1975 code for duplicate is promulgated by the World Bridge Federation, advised by the bodies enumerated above. The official Laws are published in Britain by Waddingtons Playing Card Co. Ltd.

LEAD OUT OF TURN

There are three situations:

1. *Opening lead out of turn.* Declarer may accept the lead, in which case dummy is laid down at once, declarer plays next, and dummy last. (If declarer inadvertently begins to spread his hand the lead *must* be accepted and dummy plays the hand.) If declarer does not accept the lead he has the same rights as are described in the next paragraph.

2. *Defender's subsequent lead out of turn.* Declarer may accept the lead. If he does not, he has the following options: if it was the turn of the other defender to lead he may either treat the card wrongly led as a *Penalty Card* or may require the other defender to lead, or not to lead, that suit; if it was the turn of the declarer or dummy to lead, he may either treat the card as a penalty card or may require the other defender, when first on lead, to lead, or not lead, that suit. (When the card is not treated as a penalty card it is picked up.)

3. *Declarer's lead out of turn.* The defenders may accept the lead out of turn. If they do not, there is no penalty when it was the turn of a defender to lead. If declarer has led from the wrong hand, and attention is drawn by an opponent, he must, if possible, lead a card of the same suit from his own hand. Failure to do so incurs the penalty for an established revoke.

MASTER POINTS

Success in the field of tournament play is recognized by the award of Master Points. Players may aspire to a variety of august titles. Distinctions are made according to the calibre of the tournament in which success is achieved.

MATCH PLAY

This is a duplicate contest between two teams, each of four players. One pair of a team sits North–South at one table and the other pair sits East–West at another table, preferably in a separate room. The other team occupies the opposing positions.

An agreed number of boards is played at one table and a similar number at the other table. Then the two sets of boards are exchanged and replayed, and the scores compared on each board. For methods of determining the result, see *Board-a-Match Scoring* and *International Match Points*.

A match between two teams-of-four is the simplest form of duplicate tournament and, as a test of skill, the fairest.

MISSING CARD

See *Defective Trick*.

MITCHELL MOVEMENT

This is the simplest of all movements for a pairs contest. Half the pairs sit North–South throughout the contest and half East–West. Since a pair's score can be fairly compared only with other pairs playing in the same direction, there are two winners, the top North–South pair and the top East–West.

For an odd number of tables

The Mitchell movement works best for an odd number of tables. Suppose that there are 14 pairs, forming seven tables, and that it is intended to play 28 boards. Seven pairs sit North–South and seven East–West. The first set of boards, numbers one to four, is placed on table one, the second set on table two, and so on. The players take as their pair number the number of the table at which they first sit. The first round of the tournament is then played.

When the first round is over, the North–South pairs remain stationary and the East–West pairs move up one table, from one to two, and from seven to one. The boards are moved in the reverse direction, from two to one, and from one to seven. A similar movement of boards and players is repeated at the end of each round and at the finish all the players will have played all the boards and each North–South pair will have played against each East–West pair.

For an even number of tables

The method described above will not work for an even number of tables, as the players will encounter boards which they have already played. The 'skip' method is one way of dealing with an even number of tables. Suppose there are eight. Nine sets of boards are used, not eight. On the first round the first eight sets are placed on tables one to eight and the ninth set is placed on a stand-table between tables eight and one.

At the end of the first round the movement proceeds in the ordinary way. The North–South pairs remain stationary, the East–West pairs move up one table, and the boards move down one table. The set of boards from table one goes to the stand-table, and the ninth set goes from the stand-table to table eight.

This movement continues for four rounds. On the next round the movement of the boards is the same as before, but the East–West pairs skip a table, moving from three to five, from eight to two, and so on.

A consequence of this movement is that each pair misses one set of boards. Also each North–South pair misses one East–West pair and plays twice against another. These are not serious disadvantages, but they can be avoided by using the 'relay' method.

In the 'relay' method the two end tables, one and eight, share boards throughout. Suppose again that there are eight tables. In this method eight sets of boards are in play. On the first round the first four sets are placed on tables one to four, the fifth set on a stand-table between tables four and five, and the other sets on tables five, six and seven. No boards are placed on table eight, which shares with table one.

Using the Mitchell principle, the East–West pairs move up at the end of each round and the boards move down. The only difference is that the stand-table is included in the movement of the boards, just as if it were table four and a half, and at no time is a set of boards placed on table eight at the beginning of a round.

PAIRS CONTEST

In this form of duplicate tournament each board is scored separately and the results of all the pairs who have played it in the same direction, North–South or East–West, are compared.

Suppose there are seven tables. The North–South pair that does best will score 6 points, 1 for each North–South pair whose score it has bettered. The next North–South pair will score 5 points, and so on, the pair that does worst scoring 0. When pairs have the same score, the points are shared. Two pairs who tied for first on the board would score $5\frac{1}{2}$ points each. (In Britain and some other countries the scoring is 2 for a win, 1 for a tie, to eliminate fractions.)

It follows that the East–West opponents on each hand will obtain the score that is a complement to that of their North–South opponents. When North–South score a top, their opponents score a bottom.

The special effect of match-point scoring, as it is called, is that each board carries the same number of points. Thus, part-score hands are exalted to the same level of importance as slam hands. Big swings play a smaller part, and to that extent the influence of skill is greater.

In match-point pairs both bidding and play are extremely keen, each pair striving on every hand for a slight advantage that will carry a much higher reward than, say, a couple of overtricks at total points scoring.

PAR CONTEST

This is a way of playing bridge against bogey. A number of hands containing problems in bidding and play are prepared in advance and are played by all competing pairs. After the auction the players are awarded 'par' points for reaching the best contract. Whatever the result of the auction may have been, the hand has to be played in a 'directed' contract. Points are then awarded for good play and defence. The players compare results not with one another but with par.

PASS OUT OF TURN

There are three situations to consider. The first is a pass out of turn before anyone has made a positive bid:

South	West	North	East
Pass		Pass	

Here North is the offender. The bidding reverts to West and North must pass on the first round.

The next situation is a pass when it was the turn of the right-hand opponent:

South	West	North	East
1 ♠	1 NT		Pass

The penalty is the same as above—East must pass on this round.
The third situation is a pass when it was partner's turn to call:

South	West	North	East
1 ♡			Pass

Here East must pass throughout; West may pass or bid at this turn, but may not double (or redouble); and if West passes and subsequently has the opening lead, declarer may require or forbid the lead of a specified suit.

PENALTY CARD

A card improperly exposed by a defender (and in some cases a card exposed during the auction; see *Exposed Card*) becomes a penalty card. A card exposed by declarer or dummy never becomes a penalty card.

A penalty card must be left face up on the table and must be led or played at the first opportunity. If the partner of a player who has a penalty card showing has the lead, he may be required or forbidden to lead that suit; the penalty card is then picked up. When a defender has two or more penalty cards on the table, the declarer may require him to play any one.

If a defender who has a penalty card showing attempts to lead or play another card, such card becomes an additional penalty card.

PENALTY SATISFIED OR FORFEITED

In general, when a player is unable to comply with a penalty—for example, if he has none of the suit he is required to lead—the penalty requirement is satisfied.

The penalty is forfeited if the player to the offender's left calls or plays before a legal penalty has been stated and imposed, or if partners consult about the imposition of a penalty.

Duplicate Law

The director should always be called. Players have not the right to assess or waive penalties.

PLAYED CARD

A card is played by a defender when held so that partner can see its face; by declarer when held face up near the surface of the table; by dummy when touched (except to adjust); and by any player when named.

PREMATURE LEAD OR PLAY

When a defender leads to the next trick before his partner has played to the current trick, or on the current trick plays in front of his partner, declarer may require the offender's partner to play his highest or lowest card of the suit led or to play a card from another specified suit. These options are alternative, not consecutive; see *Penalty Satisfied or Forfeited.*

A defender who plays out of turn after declarer has played from both hands is not subject to penalty, but this should not be done deliberately.

PROPRIETIES

Specifically unfair practices are discussed under *Ethics.* The following practices are objectionable and any player has a right to object to them:
1. Picking up the cards before the deal has been completed.
2. As dummy, exchanging cards with declarer before the play

(though this practice is accepted in certain circles), or leaning over to look at a defender's cards.

3. Failing to stack the tricks tidily.

4. Detaching cards from the hand before the player's turn to play (especially when declarer may be contemplating a finesse).

5. Preparing to lead to the next trick before the current trick has been completed.

6. Any form of censorious comment; we all play as well as we can.

7. Playing with speed to trap an opponent into error, the commonest mark of a low professional.

QUITTED TRICK

See *Inspection of Tricks*.

REDEAL

There must be a redeal if the deal is imperfect or a card is faced or a player picks up the wrong hand or the wrong number of cards. A redeal may be demanded (till the deal has been completed) if the deal is out of turn or the pack has not been properly cut.

REVIEW OF BIDDING

A player may ask for a (comprehensive) review of the auction at his own turn or at the end of the auction. Strictly, only an opponent may give the review. The right to ask for a review lapses for a defender after the opening lead, for declarer after dummy has gone down. Subsequently a player may ask what the contract is and whether it has been doubled or redoubled, but not by whom.

Duplicate Law

Same, except that the right to ask for a review extends till any player's first turn to play. (This is the least known and least observed of all provisions in the duplicate code.)

It has become the practice in the higher ranges of tournament play for the leader's partner to be debarred from asking for a review at the end of the auction until his partner has selected his lead and placed it face down on the table.

REVOKE CORRECTED

Any player, including dummy, may ask partner or an opponent whether his play constitutes a revoke.

If aware of it in time (see *Revoke Established*) a player must substitute a legal card. The card withdrawn, if from a defender's unfaced hand, then becomes a *Penalty Card*. A player from the non-offending side may without penalty change any card played after the revoke.

A revoke on the twelfth trick never becomes established and must be corrected. An opponent may require the offender's partner, if he played after the revoke, to play either one of his two cards.

REVOKE ESTABLISHED

A revoke (not on the twelfth trick) becomes established when either player of the offending side leads or plays to the next trick or makes a claim or concession. The right to claim a revoke lapses after all players have abandoned their hands.

When a revoke has been established, up to two tricks are transferred at the end of the play, counting for all purposes as though won in play; but no trick won before the revoke trick is transferred and there is no penalty for a subsequent revoke in the same suit, nor for any revoke when a legal card was visible on the table.

For other occasions when the penalty for an established revoke may be applicable, see *Dummy's Rights* and *Lead out of Turn*.

Duplicate Law

Only one trick is transferred, not two, but the director may assign an adjusted score if he considers the penalty inadequate. Right to claim a revoke lapses after either player of the non-offending side has made a call on the next deal or after the round has ended.

SCORING

The details of the scoring table for rubber bridge are as follows:

Trick score below the line

For each odd trick (beyond the 'book' of six tricks) in diamonds or clubs, score 20 points; in spades or hearts, 30; for the first trick at notrumps, 40; for each subsequent trick, 30.

When a doubled contract is made, these amounts are doubled. When a redoubled contract is made, they are multiplied by four.

Game is 100.

Bonus for doubled and redoubled contracts

In addition to the points scored in other ways, there is a bonus of 50 whenever a doubled or redoubled contract is fulfilled.

Overtricks

Undoubled, vulnerable or not, the simple trick value is scored above the line.

Doubled, not vulnerable, 100 is scored for each overtrick. Vulnerable, 200 for each overtrick. Redoubled, twice those figures.

Penalties for undertricks

Not vulnerable, 50 a trick. Doubled, 100 for the first undertrick, 200 for each subsequent one; redoubled, twice that.

Vulnerable, 100 each trick. Doubled, 200 for the first undertrick, 300 for each subsequent one; redoubled, twice that.

Slams

Small slam, not vulnerable, 500; vulnerable, 750. Grand slam not vulnerable, 1,000; vulnerable, 1,500.

Game and rubber bonus

For a rubber won in two games, 700. For a rubber won at game all, 500.

Honours

Held in one hand by any player, four honours in the trump suit, 100; all five, 150. For four aces at notrumps, 150.

Unfinished rubber

A side that is a game ahead scores 300. A side that has a part-score in an unfinished game scores 50.

Correcting the score

An error in keeping the score can be corrected at any time before the rubber score has been agreed upon.

There is technical exception if all players make a mistake in an entry below the line. That error may not be corrected after the end of the second succeeding deal unless there is majority consent.

For variations in duplicate play, see *Duplicate Scoring*.

SCREENS

In important tournaments diagonal screens may be placed across the table during the bidding so that the players can see an opponent but not partner. Bids are written down (or otherwise silently indicated) and are either announced by officials or circulated round the table. In theory, though not always in practice, players will be unable to tell who on the other side of the screen has paused for thought.

SIMULTANEOUS CALL

A call made simultaneously with that of another player is deemed to have been made after it and may if irregular attract the penalty for an *Insufficient Bid* or for a *Bid, Double or Redouble out of Turn*.

SIMULTANEOUS LEAD OR PLAY

A lead or play made simultaneously with a correct lead or play is deemed to have been made after it and may attract a penalty. If a defender leads or plays two cards simultaneously, the card he does not designate as the correct one becomes a *Penalty Card*.

SKIP BID

After a pre-emptive bid, such as an opening three hearts, the next player may find it difficult to make his call in normal tempo and may therefore convey some information to his partner. To prevent this, tournament players are required to call 'Stop' or 'Skip bid', warning the next player to pause for several seconds, whatever his hand. It is becoming quite common for this form of warning to be advised not just for pre-empts but for all jump bids.

See also *Alert Procedure*.

SURPLUS CARD

See *Defective Trick*.

SWISS MOVEMENT

This is a popular movement for multiple team events. Its special feature is that a complete set of rankings is produced after each round and forms the basis for the draw in the next round. The top team plays the second team, the third team plays the fourth team, and so on.

TOURNAMENT BRIDGE

All tournament bridge is played according to the 'duplicate' principle: a hand that has been dealt and played at one table is preserved and played again at one or more other tables, with the same dealer and vulnerability. The luck of the deal is in a sense eliminated and a direct comparison of skill can be made.

During the play of the hand the cards are not played into the centre of the table. Each player puts his own cards face downward at his side of the table. When the play is finished, each player's hand is put in a separate slot of a container called a 'duplicate board', which at the end of a round is transferred to another table. The players are designated North, South, East and West. The vulnerability conditions and the position of the dealer are shown on the board.

Scoring is somewhat different from rubber bridge. See *Duplicate Scoring*.

There are two main kinds of tournament: team-of-four games (see *Match Play*) and pairs tournaments. Tournaments are conducted at every level from the local bridge club to the world championships organized by the World Bridge Federation.

Tournament bridge has its own code of laws, called 'The Laws of Duplicate Contract Bridge', standard throughout the world.

UNAUTHORIZED INFORMATION DURING BIDDING

Suppose a player makes such a remark as 'Why didn't you give me a chance to double?' Either opponent may require both the offender and his partner to pass thereafter, and declarer may require the offender's partner, when first he has the lead, to lead, or not to lead, a specified suit. See also *Changing a Call*.

Duplicate Law

The director should be summoned forthwith. He will normally rule that play continue and may afterwards assign an adjusted score.

UNAUTHORIZED INFORMATION DURING PLAY

If a defender makes some remark conveying improper information, or dummy says, for example, 'Why don't you draw trumps?', an opponent may at any time subsequent to the offence, but once only, prohibit the offender's partner from making the lead or play improperly suggested.

In the event of unauthorized information about a single card, this card may become a *Penalty Card*.

Duplicate Law

The director should be summoned forthwith. He will normally rule that play continue and may afterwards assign an adjusted score.

VU-GRAPH

The successor to *Bridgerama*, Vu-Graph employs the magic lantern principle to enable an audience to follow the play. The deals are inscribed on 'transparencies' whose image is thrown on a screen. As cards are played, they are ticked off on the transparencies.

YARBOROUGH

A term descended from the game of whist, meaning a hand that contains no card above a 9.

The name comes from a former Earl of Yarborough, who offered to bet any whist player £1,000 to £1 that he would not pick up such a hand on a given deal. Since the true odds are 1,827 to 1, his lordship appears to have been a shrewd operator.